THE REVISED VERSION
EDITED FOR THE USE OF SCHOOLS

THE

BOOK OF GENESIS

I—XXIV

T0364319

THE
BOOK OF GENESIS
I—XXIV

BY

H. C. O. LANCHESTER, M.A.

RECTOR OF FRAMLINGHAM, SUFFOLK

FORMERLY FELLOW OF PEMBROKE COLLEGE, CAMBRIDGE

CAMBRIDGE

AT THE UNIVERSITY PRESS

1923

CAMBRIDGE
UNIVERSITY PRESS

University Printing House, Cambridge CB2 8BS, United Kingdom

Published in the United States of America by Cambridge University Press, New York

Cambridge University Press is part of the University of Cambridge.

It furthers the University's mission by disseminating knowledge in the pursuit of education, learning and research at the highest international levels of excellence.

www.cambridge.org
Information on this title: www.cambridge.org/9781107652712

© Cambridge University Press 1923

First published 1923
First paperback edition 2014

A catalogue record for this publication is available from the British Library

ISBN 978-1-107-65271-2 Paperback

Additional resources for this publication at www.cambridge.org/9781107652712

PREFACE BY THE GENERAL EDITOR
FOR THE OLD TESTAMENT

THE aim of this series of commentaries is to explain the Revised Version for young students, and at the same time to present, in a simple form, the main results of the best scholarship of the day.

The General Editor has confined himself to supervision and suggestion. The writer is, in each case, responsible for the opinions expressed and for the treatment of particular passages.

A. H. M^cNEILE.

March, 1923.

CONTENTS

MAP

*available for download in colour from www.cambridge.org/9781107652712

INTRODUCTION

1. Name.

GENESIS is a Greek word meaning 'generation' or 'coming into being.' It is the title of the book found in the LXX, and it is derived from the Greek of ii. 4, 'These are the generations of the heaven and of the earth,' or, as the LXX has it, 'This is the book of the genesis of the heaven and of the earth.' In the Hebrew the title is derived, as often, from the first word (or words) of the book: it is Bᵉrēshīth, 'In the Beginning.' The Greek title passed through the Latin into common use, the only serious rival being 'the first book of Moses.' According to the ancient, but unscientific, tradition, the first five books of the Old Testament were composed by Moses.

2. Scope.

Neither Genesis nor Bᵉrēshīth is a satisfactory title for the whole book, for each describes only the opening chapters. We are brought back, not so far indeed as in the opening words of St John's Gospel, but to the beginning of time, and the panorama of Creation is gradually unfolded before our eyes. Then the history of primitive man is sketched from his Creation, through the Fall and the subsequent deterioration of man, to the Flood. Then man is represented as making a fresh start in the persons of Noah and his family, and so we get to the divisions of nations and the origin of the diversity of languages. With xi. 27 a new section begins, leading up to the call of Abram and the history of the patriarchs.

3. Sources.

In studying any history it is always important to discover as far as possible to what sources the historian has had access. The book of Genesis is not a history in the modern sense, for it deals with a very wide period of time in which, for obvious reasons, historical records could not be kept. Nor is it the work of a single author. The old Jewish tradition that Moses himself wrote the first five books of the Bible has been abandoned by all serious scholars. Rather we may look for the first beginnings of the book to ancient traditions handed down, as they are so often in the East, by word of mouth from generation to generation. Some of these traditions, perhaps the earliest of them, would be couched in poetry, and scattered throughout the book we find many poetical pieces of varying length, e.g. iv. 23 f., v. 29, ix. 25–27, xvi. 11 f., xxv. 23, xxvii. 27–29, 39 f., xlix. 2–27. Most primitive nations have their own collections of folk-lore, dealing with such things as the beginnings of the world, the relations of mankind with the world of nature, and the origins of manners and customs. Such folk-lore stories have come down to us in some of the early narratives of Genesis, and it is very interesting to compare them with the legends of other people. Then again tribes and families have their own traditions, which tell them of their past and inspire them to maintain their heritage.

All these sources enter into the composition of the book of Genesis, but they do not in themselves explain the book as it has come down to us. If this was all that Genesis contained, it would be deeply interesting from an antiquarian point of view, but its religious value would be very slight. What makes all the difference to us is that we recognize behind the book the inspiration of God, not in the sense that thereby every detail is rendered literally or scientifically correct, but in the sense that we feel that all the different strata have been welded together into a book which God has used to shew forth His works, and to reveal His dealings among men.

How did these traditions, folk-lore stories and other elements come to be put together? This question cannot be answered with reference to Genesis alone: we must take into account all the five books of the Pentateuch, or, as most scholars would include the book of Joshua, of the Hexateuch (the *six volume* collection).

When we pick up a book, unless anything is said to the contrary, we usually assume it to be the work of one author. But if, on closer inspection, we find narratives repeated with different details, contradictions between one part and another, a different way of looking at things in different sections, and finally a variety of language and style, we are driven to the conclusion that the author has combined different sources without succeeding in welding them into an entirely homogeneous whole. A careful inspection shews that this must have happened in the case of Genesis, and indeed of the Hexateuch as a whole. The credit of first arriving at this conclusion, which has found acceptance with nearly all reputable scholars, is due to Jean Astruc, a French physician practising at Brussels, who published his studies in 1753. Since that date scholars of many nations have examined the books of the Hexateuch with the minutest care, and from their studies certain general results have emerged which are more or less universally accepted.

Briefly four strands or sources have been disentangled which are conventionally known as J, E, D, and P. The first two letters refer to sources which shew a preference for different forms of the Divine Name: one using Jehovah (or Yahweh), which is rendered 'the LORD,' while the other has Elohim = God. P denotes the Priestly source, so called because it shews marked affinities with the language and standpoint of the Priests from Ezekiel onwards; while D, which hardly comes into account in Genesis, displays the very marked and individual style of Deuteronomy.

4. CHARACTERISTICS OF THE SOURCES.

It would take far too long to work out in detail the marks by which these several sources can be detected, but it is possible to give certain broad outlines by which characteristic passages may be recognized.

P is the easiest source to distinguish. We note orderliness of arrangement, constantly recurrent words and phrases, such as 'these are the generations,' 'after their kind,' 'these are the names of,' 'covenant,' etc., a fondness for genealogies, dates, numbers and figures as in the dimensions of the ark and the rise and fall of the waters. Typical P passages are i.–ii. 3, ix. 1–17, xvii.

J and E are not so readily distinguished from each other, apart from their characteristic uses of the Divine Name. J is perhaps preeminent for his antiquarian interests, e.g. the institution of marriage (ii. 24), the origin of sacrifice (iv. 3 f.), of agriculture (iv. 20), music (21), and craftsmanship (22). His narrative is most picturesque and vivid. God is regularly called Jehovah (the LORD), and He is represented continually as performing the actions of men: e.g. He walks in the Garden of Eden (iii. 8), shuts Noah into the ark (vii. 16), smells the savour of the sacrifice (viii. 21), and comes down to see the tower of Babel (xi. 5). Obviously this represents a primitive idea of God. In E, on the other hand, God's messages to men are conveyed by means of a vision (xv. 1), or a dream (xx. 3, 6), or by an angel (xxi. 17, xxii. 11). He does not intervene personally. E has not as a rule the freshness and picturesqueness of J, but the matchless narrative of ch. xxii. is assigned to him.

A very little practice enables the student to distinguish without much difficulty a passage of P from a passage of J. He cannot, for instance, fail to recognize the difference of atmosphere between the stately, methodical, and somewhat stereotyped narrative of Genesis i.–ii. 4ª and the fresh, vigorous, and naïve description of ii. 4ᵇ–end. But there are many passages in which the two kinds of styles seem to be so mixed up that we must conclude that someone has made a conflate narrative out of both. This is especially noticeable in the story of the Flood in ch. viii. In the same way J and E are sometimes conflated, as at the beginning of ch. xv.

So we get the following outline of stages by which the book of Genesis appears to have reached its present form.

First the ancient stories were collected and committed to writing by the author known as J, who lived in the Southern Kingdom somewhere about 850 B.C. A little more than half a century later another collection was made by someone living in the Northern Kingdom known as E. These two narratives were combined perhaps in the 7th century (J, E), J forming the ground-work. Then, during the Exile in the 6th century, the old history was re-written from a somewhat different standpoint by a school of men whose training and outlook were similar to that of Ezekiel: this we find in P. Finally J, E, and P were welded together somewhere in the 5th century to form the book which we have now. One chapter (xiv.) appears to stand outside any of the sources mentioned above, and it is not known from whence it is derived.

5. THE EARLY NARRATIVES AND BABYLONIA.

We have seen that many of the stories in Genesis are based on traditions handed down from remote antiquity. Discoveries in Babylonia, and especially the decipherment of the ancient language of that country, have given a great deal of additional interest to these stories, because they shew us that the Babylonians had traditions of early times which are in many ways strikingly similar to those which we find in Genesis. Indeed it is probable that the Biblical accounts rest ultimately on these primitive Babylonian traditions, but they have been purged of their polytheism and grotesque features, and are presented in a form that is full of religious teaching.

For example, there is a Babylonian account of Creation, preserved in tablets which came from the Library of Asshurbanipal at Nineveh. This account starts with a watery chaos (Tiamat) at the beginning of all, and describes how first of all the gods were created from Apsu and Tiamat. Then follows a contest between Tiamat and these gods, whose champion was Marduk, in the course of which Marduk catches Tiamat in his net and splits her asunder, one half forming the sky and the other the earth. Then the sun and moon are created, and finally man. The tablets are incomplete, and the rest of Creation was probably recorded in the missing parts.

The Babylonian story of the Flood is given in the following form by Utnapishtim to Gilgamesh, who has succeeded in crossing the waters of Death, and finds Utnapishtim standing on the further shore.

The gods determine to destroy the city of Shurippak by a great flood, and Ea warns Utnapishtim to escape by building a great ship, into which he is to bring the seed of life of every sort. The ship is duly built in seven stories and made watertight by pitch. Then Utnapishtim takes in his family, servants, and possessions, and all kinds of animals, and the door is shut. For six days the rain falls and the earth is covered. Then Utnapishtim sends out successively a dove and a swallow which return to him, and finally a raven which does not return. Then he leaves the ship and offers sacrifice on the summit of the mountain.

Here the parallels are so close that the two accounts can hardly be independent. The Babylonian account is no doubt the older, but it remains to-day merely as a literary curiosity, while the Hebrew narrative has exercised a profound influence on religious thought.

Students of folk-lore have collected accounts of Creation and of a Flood, which have many affinities with the Biblical narratives, from peoples living in widely separated regions of the world. A comparison with such narratives brings out clearly the religious value of the Genesis stories quite apart from any consideration of their literal or scientific accuracy.

6. The value of Genesis.

(a) *Historical.* We have already seen that the earlier chapters rest on tradition and folk-lore rather than on sober history. Obviously no historical records would be kept in the primitive times which are there represented, and any memories of them which survived would suffer many alterations in the course of time. For instance, they would hardly avoid exaggeration. So the story of the Flood may rest ultimately on the memory of some unusual inundation in the plains of Babylon, and the story of the tower of Babel may go back to the building of some tower of considerable height in the same country.

Of course God might have revealed actual historical details to Moses, or some other man, so that the narrative would be literally true; but the more we study His words, the more certain we become that this is not His way of dealing with men. The lessons are His, but the framework of them is taken from the conditions of human life and thought.

(b) *Scientific.* The above consideration takes away the difficulties which weighed heavily upon the minds of men about the middle of last century with regard to the apparent contradiction between religion and science. Science tells us e.g. that the earth is immeasurably older than any date we can arrive at from Genesis, that the process of Creation cannot have been such as the first two chapters describe, that a flood sufficient to cover the world up to the tops of the mountains is unthinkable. We may accept these and similar conclusions without feeling that thereby Genesis has lost any of its interest or importance. These old stories are still for us the medium which God has used for teaching His eternal lessons.

(c) *Religious.* So, apart from its literary or antiquarian interest, the real value of Genesis lies in the lessons which it has to teach. It tells us that the world in which we live and everything in it, small or great, is the handiwork of God the Creator: that without sin the world is very beautiful and very good: that sin is the great destroyer of happiness, and that it arises from allowing suggestions of evil to find an entrance into our hearts: that sin inevitably leads to punishment, and that the worst punishment is estrangement from God: that evil grows apace in this world and ultimately leads to disaster: that God's purposes are never quite frustrated though they seem sometimes to suffer long delays, and that from the very beginning He was preparing the world so that in the fulness of time He might send into it His Son. This preparation took the form of choosing a man, from whom a nation should ultimately be derived, which He should use for the religious education of the world, and out of which Christ should arise.

Apart from these main outlines the religious or moral interest may be traced in almost every narrative and in the delineation of character. It is true that the religious ideas are not always such as would commend themselves to us, but they were at least abreast of the spirit of their age, and they mark definite steps in the education of the religious faculty in man.

7. The Conception of God.

As has been indicated above, we have three different strata of ideas about God contained in the three main sources. In the earliest He is represented as acting and speaking very much as a mighty human monarch. He walks and talks with men, makes plans to circumvent man's growing pride or influence, is pleased with the smell of a sacrifice, and works by certain laws which sometimes seem to us arbitrary. In this source the human interest is always emphasized. In the somewhat later source E, He is farther removed from men, and His will is conveyed by means of dreams and visions. In the Priestly source (P) there are stages in the revelation of God to men: first he is God (Elohim), then God Almighty (El Shaddai), and finally, only in the time of Moses, Jehovah. His relation to man is sometimes described under the figure of a covenant as though He were the Great Lawyer. The idea underlying this is a true one and of permanent value, for it emphasizes the necessity of man's response to the privileges which God offers to him: but it can easily be made too rigid and automatic. There is not wanting in P the 'larger hope' that Israel may be used to spread God's blessings over all the nations of the earth.

Taking these different conceptions of God together, we have a study of exceptional interest. For we see that the religious education of mankind was akin to that of a little child: that simple thoughts came first, and that errors and misunderstandings were corrected, and the teaching broadened and deepened as the mind of man was able to bear it.

8. The Faith of Abraham.

Jewish history begins with the figure of Abraham, the great ancestor of the nation (cf. Matt. iii. 9; John viii. 33, 53; Rom. iv. 1, xi. i.). His is the first full-length portrait in the gallery of the Old Testament, and he shares with

Moses and David the distinction of being the most famous of the heroes of the nation. He is preeminently the great example of faith, and the father of the faithful (Rom. iv. 12).

There were two main occasions on which this faith was displayed; first when he obeyed God's command to go forth from his own country to an unknown land (Gen. xv. 4; Hebr. xi. 8), and secondly when he was prepared to offer up his only true son Isaac as a sacrifice (Gen. xxii. 10; Hebr. xi. 17). In each case faith manifested itself in obedience; but it was not mere passive obedience, but rather the intuitive assurance that God was working out a plan, the details of which Abraham was content to leave, for the time, entirely obscure. So his obedience rested on a whole-hearted belief in God—His wisdom, and His power and His love. Jewish theologians laid particular stress on his being the first monotheist, i.e. the first to believe absolutely in God as one and supreme. They contrast the atmosphere of polytheism in which he lived all the earlier part of his life, both Ur and Haran being centres of the worship of the moon-god. It was this splendid faith that evoked the promise that he should be a source of blessing to all the nations of the world (xxii. 18), and that earned him the title of the Friend of God (Isa. xli. 8), which is still perpetuated by the Arabic name of Hebron, 'el Khalil' (the friend). Yet Abraham's character was not a perfect one, and the story of how he denied his wife in Egypt (xii. 13) is a reminder that great men have their falls sometimes. To the writer in Genesis it was probably significant that this lapse took place in Egypt. In the land of promise he was strong, but in the unclean land of Egypt his faith for a time gave way.

9. ABRAHAM'S HOME.

The site of Ur of the Chaldees, the original home of Abraham, was first identified in 1854 by Sir Henry

Rawlinson, but it is only in the last few years, after the interest aroused by the Mesopotamian campaign, that serious excavations have been attempted. An account of the discoveries made at Ur during last winter by the expedition sent out by the British Museum and the University Museum of Pennsylvania was given in an article in the *Times* of July 16, 1923.

It is well known that in ancient times the Persian Gulf extended very much further to the north than it does to-day, the silt brought down by the Euphrates and Tigris having gradually reclaimed many miles of sea. It appears that in Abraham's time Ur was almost a sea-side town, and indeed formed a principal port of Babylonia. It was, like Antwerp, the great emporium through which the sea-borne trade to and from Arabia, Babylonia, Elam and other countries passed. So it was a large and wealthy city, and it contained two great temples to Sin the moon-god, served by numerous priests, who grew rich on the offerings made by the merchants. Here Abraham lived at the time of the city's greatest prosperity, shortly before Hammurabi materially reduced its wealth and influence by the refounding of Babylon. If Abraham was himself a prosperous merchant, owning numerous servants and camels, and sending his caravans along the trade routes into distant lands, it makes his faith all the more striking that at God's command he should leave the comfort and civilization of life in a great city, to become a dweller in tents and a sojourner in a land that was not his. The Epistle to the Hebrews sees in him one who 'looked for the city which hath the foundations, whose builder and maker is God' (xi. 10).

It is not improbable that further excavations at Ur may throw fresh light on Abraham's history. What has already been done has made it easier for us to picture the conditions under which the earlier part of his life was passed.

10. The Early Chapters of Genesis in the New Testament.

No part of the Old Testament is so often referred to in the New Testament as the first half of Genesis, and the following list of references is not intended to be exhaustive.

	GENESIS	NEW TESTAMENT
i.	1. Creation ...	Acts xvii. 24, Hebr. xi. 3, Rev. iv. 11, x. 6
	27. Male and female created he them	Matt. xix. 4, Mk x. 6
ii.	9. Tree of life	Rev. xxii. 2
	24. A man shall...cleave unto his wife...one flesh	Matt. xix. 5, Mk x. 7, 1 Cor. vi.16, Eph. v. 31
iii.	1-21. The Fall	Rom. v. 14, 1 Cor. xv. 22, 1 Tim. ii. 13-15
	17. Adam	1 Cor. xv. 22, 45
iv.	4. Abel's sacrifice	Hebr. xi. 4
	8. Cain	1 John iii. 12, Jude 11
	10. Abel's death	Lk. xi. 51, Hebr. xii. 24
v.	24. Enoch	Hebr. xi. 5, Jude 14
vi.	4. Fallen angels	Jude 6, Rev. xii. 9
	9 ff. Noah	Matt. xxiv. 37–39, Lk. xvii. 26–27, Hebr. xi. 7, 1 Pet. iii. 20, 2 Pet. ii. 5
xi.	26 etc. Abraham (many references)	John viii. *passim* and elsewhere
xii.	1. migration of	Acts vii. 2 ff, Hebr. xi. 8
	2, 3 etc. promises to	Lk. i. 55, 73, Acts iii. 25, Hebr. vi. 14
xiv.	18. Melchizedek	Hebr. v. 6, 10, vii. *passim*
xv.	6. Abraham, faith of	Rom. iv., Gal. iii. 6 ff, Hebr. xi. 8, Jas. ii. 21
xvii.	11. Circumcision	Acts vii. 8, Rom. ii. 25 ff and elsewhere
xix.	Lot	Lk. xvii. 28, 2 Pet. ii. 7
	24-25. Sodom and Gomorrah	Lk. xvii. 29, Rom. ix. 29, 2 Pet. ii. 6, Jude 7, Rev. xi. 8
	26. Lot's wife	Lk. xvii. 32
xxi.	2. Sarah	Hebr. xi. 11, 1 Pet. iii. 6
	3. Abraham, birth of Isaac	Rom. ix. 7 ff.
	8-12. Isaac and Ishmael	Gal. iv. 21-31
xxii.	Offering of Isaac ...	Hebr. xi. 17, Jas. ii. 21

II. ANALYSIS.

THE FIRST BOOK OF MOSES,

COMMONLY CALLED

GENESIS

i.–ii. 4ᵃ. *The story of Creation as told in the later source, P.*

In the beginning God created the heaven and the earth. **1**
And the earth was waste and void ; and darkness was upon **2**
the face of the deep : and the spirit of God moved upon
the face of the waters.

3–5. (1) *Light.*

And God said, Let there be light : and there was light. **3**
And God saw the light, that it was good : and God divided **4**

---

i.–ii. 4a. The world and all that is in it comes into being by an
orderly succession of creative acts divided into six days.

i. 1. In the beginning : i.e. of time as we know it. In John
i. 1 the expression goes back infinitely beyond this.

God created. The first thought of God which the Bible contains is that of Creator. He created all things by His word
(Ps. xxxiii. 6). Other peoples had conceived of the world as
coming into being through the strife of opposing forces of divine
nature. But 'dualism' of this kind finds no place in primitive
Hebrew thought.

2. waste and void : is chaotic and formless. God's task was
not so much to create out of nothing, as to give form and order
to chaos.

the spirit of God. The spirit of God is His creative energy,
cf. Ps. civ. 30.

moved : the verb is used again only in Deut. xxxii. 11 (R.V.
fluttereth). It has been supposed to allude to the old myth that
the world was created by the hatching of a primeval egg.

3. light : regarded as existing before the heavenly bodies,
cf. Job xxxviii. 19, though later gathered up and concentrated
in them. Light is the first requisite for all order and progress.

5 the light from the darkness. And God called the light
Day, and the darkness he called Night. And there was
evening and there was morning, one day.

6-8. (2) *Firmament.*

6 And God said, Let there be a firmament in the midst
of the waters, and let it divide the waters from the waters.
7 And God made the firmament, and divided the waters
which were under the firmament from the waters which
8 were above the firmament: and it was so. And God called
the firmament Heaven. And there was evening and there
was morning, a second day.

9-13. (3) *Land, sea, and vegetation.*

9 And God said, Let the waters under the heaven be
gathered together unto one place, and let the dry land
10 appear: and it was so. And God called the dry land
Earth; and the gathering together of the waters called he
11 Seas: and God saw that it was good. And God said, Let
the earth put forth grass, herb yielding seed, *and* fruit tree
bearing fruit after its kind, wherein is the seed thereof,
12 upon the earth: and it was so. And the earth brought
forth grass, herb yielding seed after its kind, and tree
bearing fruit, wherein is the seed thereof, after its kind:

---

5. one day: obviously not historically a day of 24 hours as
we know it. Each 'day' marks in a picturesque way a separate
stage in the order of creation.

6. a firmament: cf. Ps. xix. 1, cl. 1; Ezek. i. 22 ff. The
Hebrews conceived of the sky as an arch of molten metal, resting
on high hills at the four corners of the earth (cf. Job xxvi. 11).
Above this firmament were the stores of waters which came down
in the form of rain.

9. let the dry land appear: apparently the land is conceived
of as already in existence but sunk beneath the waters (cf. Ps.
xxiv. 2). The earth, of course, is regarded as a flat surface.

11. Three kinds of produce are specified in an ascending scale:
grass for the cattle, herb, i.e. cereals, vegetables etc., and fruit
trees. For the first two cf. Ps. civ. 14.

and God saw that it was good. And there was evening 13
and there was morning, a third day.

14–19. (4) *Sun, moon, and stars.*

And God said, Let there be lights in the firmament of 14
the heaven to divide the day from the night; and let them
be for signs, and for seasons, and for days and years: and 15
let them be for lights in the firmament of the heaven
to give light upon the earth: and it was so. And God 16
made the two great lights; the greater light to rule the
day, and the lesser light to rule the night: *he made* the
stars also. And God set them in the firmament of the 17
heaven to give light upon the earth, and to rule over the 18
day and over the night, and to divide the light from the
darkness: and God saw that it was good. And there was 19
evening and there was morning, a fourth day.

20–23. (5) *Fish and fowl.*

And God said, Let the waters bring forth abundantly 20
the moving creature that hath life, and let fowl fly above
the earth in the open firmament of heaven. And God 21
created the great sea-monsters, and every living creature
that moveth, which the waters brought forth abundantly,

---

14. The purpose of the lights of heaven is described as three-
fold: (1) to divide day and night, (2) to divide the seasons, (3) to
give light.

16. to rule the day: cf. Ps. cxxxvi. 8 f. The sun is regarded
as a kind of king. Compare the somewhat different thought in
Ps. xix. 5.

20–23. The list of animate creations is given in ascending
order as in the Benedicite.

20. bring forth abundantly: the reference is to the shoals of
fish and aquatic animals that swarm in the sea.

fowl: not merely birds but all creatures that fly.

21. sea-monsters. Such played a considerable part in the
imagination of primitive man. The Hebrews called the largest
of these Leviathan, which in Ps. civ. 26 seems to mean the whale,
and in Job xli. the crocodile.

after their kinds, and every winged fowl after its kind:
22 and God saw that it was good. And God blessed them,
saying, Be fruitful, and multiply, and fill the waters in the
23 seas, and let fowl multiply in the earth. And there was
evening and there was morning, a fifth day.

24–31. (6) *Beasts and man.*

24 And God said, Let the earth bring forth the living
creature after its kind, cattle, and creeping thing, and beast
25 of the earth after its kind: and it was so. And God made
the beast of the earth after its kind, and the cattle after
their kind, and every thing that creepeth upon the ground
26 after its kind: and God saw that it was good. And God
said, Let us make man in our image, after our likeness:
and let them have dominion over the fish of the sea, and
over the fowl of the air, and over the cattle, and over all
the earth, and over every creeping thing that creepeth
27 upon the earth. And God created man in his own image,
in the image of God created he him; male and female
28 created he them. And God blessed them: and God said
unto them, Be fruitful, and multiply, and replenish the
earth, and subdue it; and have dominion over the fish of
the sea, and over the fowl of the air, and over every living
29 thing that moveth upon the earth. And God said, Behold,
I have given you every herb yielding seed, which is upon
the face of all the earth, and every tree, in the which is the
fruit of a tree yielding seed; to you it shall be for meat:

---

26. Let us make man. The use of the plural *us* is noticeable.
The best explanation seems to be that it is the plural of Majesty,
as in our Royal Proclamations. The same use occurs again in
iii. 22, xi. 7; Isa. vi. 8. But cf. p. 95.

in our image, after our likeness. The two words, which are
to be understood as meaning the same thing, can hardly refer to
physical likeness. Man differs from the beasts as having in himself a spark of the Divine, which we call his spirit.

let them have dominion: cf. Ps. viii. 6–8.

29. for meat: an archaism for *food* found also in R.V. in

and to every beast of the earth, and to every fowl of the 30 air, and to every thing that creepeth upon the earth, wherein there is life, *I have given* every green herb for meat: and it was so. And God saw every thing that he 31 had made, and, behold, it was very good. And there was evening and there was morning, the sixth day.

ii. 1–4ᵃ. (7) *The day of rest.*

And the heaven and the earth were finished, and all the 2 host of them. And on the seventh day God finished his 2 work which he had made ; and he rested on the seventh day from all his work which he had made. And God blessed 3 the seventh day, and hallowed it: because that in it he rested from all his work which God had created and made.

These are the generations of the heaven and of the 4 earth when they were created,

4ᵇ–25. *The story of Creation as told in the earlier source, J.*

in the day that the LORD God made earth and heaven. And no plant of the field was yet in the earth, and no herb 5

---

1 Kings xix. 8; Ps. lxix. 21; Isa. lxii. 8; Joel i. 16. Man is here represented as a vegetarian. The permission to eat flesh comes first in ix. 3.

ii. 2. he rested on the seventh day. From the Hebrew verb *Shābhath* = *rested* comes the word 'Sabbath.' The same sanction for the Sabbath is given in the Fourth Commandment. If we understand the six days of Creation as metaphorical rather than literal we cannot lay stress on the form of this sanction. But the Divine institution of the Sabbath is independent of any theory as to the literal truth of the story of Creation.

4a. These are the generations. This formula which in P so often begins a section (v. 1, x. 1, xi. 10, 27) is here placed at the end.

4b–25. Here man is created before vegetation and animal life.

4b. the LORD God: the word LORD is spelt in capital letters to signify that it represents the sacred name YHWH which is usually written as Jehovah, but should more strictly be pronounced Yahweh. Reverence forbade the Jews to pronounce the name at all.

of the field had yet sprung up: for the LORD God had not
caused it to rain upon the earth, and there was not a man
6 to till the ground; but there went up a mist from the
7 earth, and watered the whole face of the ground. And the
LORD God formed man of the dust of the ground, and
breathed into his nostrils the breath of life; and man be-
8 came a living soul. And the LORD God planted a garden
eastward, in Eden; and there he put the man whom he had
9 formed. And out of the ground made the LORD God to
grow every tree that is pleasant to the sight, and good for
food; the tree of life also in the midst of the garden, and
10 the tree of the knowledge of good and evil. And a river
went out of Eden to water the garden; and from thence

---

7. of the dust of the ground: referring to man's material
body, cf. iii. 19; Job x. 9, xxxiv. 15; Ps. civ. 29; Eccl. xii. 7;
1 Cor. xv. 47.

breathed into his nostrils: man's life is regarded as an in-
breathing of the Divine life. The words refer principally to the
physical life, but they seem at least to have some reference to a
spiritual life. In vii. 22 the 'breath of life' is used in the wider
sense. In Job xxxiii. 4 human life is again regarded as a Divine
gift.

8. a garden...in Eden. From the Greek word for 'garden'
comes the word Paradise. It is derived ultimately from a Persian
word meaning 'park.' Eden means literally 'pleasure.' For
references to Eden cf. Isa. li. 3; Joel ii. 3; Ezek. xxviii. 13, xxxi.
9, 16, 18, xxxvi. 35.

9. the tree of life: i.e. the tree whose fruit gives immortality,
cf. Rev. xxii. 2. Sacred trees play an important part in ancient
mythology.

10. It is not possible to find a geographical site for Eden
which is wholly satisfactory, and therefore the rivers are also uncertain. *Euphrates* of course is clear, and *Hiddekel* refers to the
Tigris. By *Gihon* the writer may have intended the Nile which
was thought to rise somewhere in Asia, but *Pishon* is quite uncertain. The same may be said of the land of *Havilah*. *Cush* is
the Hebrew name for Ethiopia, though sometimes it seems to be
used of a district in Arabia. Some have thought that in the
description of the rivers of Eden the sacred writer had in mind
the irrigation canals of Mesopotamia, which existed at least as far
back as 2000 B.C.

it was parted, and became four heads. The name of the 11
first is Pishon: that is it which compasseth the whole land
of Havilah, where there is gold; and the gold of that land 12
is good: there is bdellium and the onyx stone. And the 13
name of the second river is Gihon: the same is it that
compasseth the whole land of Cush. And the name of the 14
third river is Hiddekel: that is it which goeth in front of
Assyria. And the fourth river is Euphrates. And the LORD 15
God took the man, and put him into the garden of Eden to
dress it and to keep it. And the LORD God commanded 16
the man, saying, Of every tree of the garden thou mayest
freely eat: but of the tree of the knowledge of good and evil, 17
thou shalt not eat of it: for in the day that thou eatest
thereof thou shalt surely die.

18–25. Creation of animals and formation of woman.

And the LORD God said, It is not good that the man 18
should be alone; I will make him an help meet for him.
And out of the ground the LORD God formed every beast 19
of the field, and every fowl of the air; and brought them
unto the man to see what he would call them: and whatsoever the man called every living creature, that was the
name thereof. And the man gave names to all cattle, and 20
to the fowl of the air, and to every beast of the field;
but for man there was not found an help meet for him.
And the LORD God caused a deep sleep to fall upon the 21
man, and he slept; and he took one of his ribs, and closed

---

17. thou shalt not eat of it. From the first man is put
under moral law, and the possibility of obeying it or not implies
free will.

18. an help meet for him: is suitable for him as a companion.
The word *helpmeet*, which sometimes takes the form *helpmate*,
is a curious instance of misunderstanding.

20. the man gave names. The names are apparently regarded
as fitting the different animals, and Hebrew is regarded as the
primitive language. The picture is perhaps that of a man making
an inventory of his new possessions.

22 up the flesh instead thereof: and the rib, which the LORD
God had taken from the man, made he a woman, and
23 brought her unto the man. And the man said, This is now
bone of my bones, and flesh of my flesh: she shall be called
24 Woman, because she was taken out of Man. Therefore
shall a man leave his father and his mother, and shall cleave
25 unto his wife: and they shall be one flesh. And they were
both naked, the man and his wife, and were not ashamed.

iii. 1–24. *The Fall of Man and his expulsion from Eden.*

3 Now the serpent was more subtil than any beast of the
field which the LORD God had made. And he said unto
the woman, Yea, hath God said, Ye shall not eat of any
2 tree of the garden? And the woman said unto the serpent,
3 Of the fruit of the trees of the garden we may eat: but of
the fruit of the tree which is in the midst of the garden,
God hath said, Ye shall not eat of it, neither shall ye touch
4 it, lest ye die. And the serpent said unto the woman, Ye

---

22. the rib...made he a woman. The description is hardly
intended to be taken literally: it describes in a figure the mutual
interdependence of man and woman, or perhaps, in closer accord
with the Hebrew outlook, the dependence of woman on man.

24. Therefore shall a man leave.... In this form the words
are a command. But they may equally well be represented by
the present tenses in English 'leaves'...'cleaves.' If so they are
the explanation of a fact. For our Lord's use of the words cf.
Matt. xix. 4–6, Mk x. 6–8.

iii. 1. the serpent. The Spirit of evil is represented by the
serpent as being the most mysterious of the creatures: primitive
man gave it the reputation of wisdom, especially in knowledge
of evil. Compare our Lord's reference in Matt. x. 16. The
name 'Satan' is much later. The story is again pictorial, and the
main lesson conveyed is that evil comes from without, working
upon the mind of man.

hath God said: the first step is to suggest that God is un-
reasonable, then, in *v.* 5, that He is jealous. It has been noticed that
in early Greek writers the jealousy of the gods is a frequent theme.

4. Ye shall not surely die: the serpent, gaining boldness from
the success of his former suggestion, now contradicts directly
God's injunction.

shall not surely die: for God doth know that in the day ye 5
eat thereof, then your eyes shall be opened, and ye shall
be as God, knowing good and evil. And when the woman 6
saw that the tree was good for food, and that it was a
delight to the eyes, and that the tree was to be desired to
make one wise, she took of the fruit thereof, and did eat;
and she gave also unto her husband with her, and he
did eat. And the eyes of them both were opened, and they 7
knew that they were naked; and they sewed fig leaves
together, and made themselves aprons. And they heard 8
the voice of the LORD God walking in the garden in the
cool of the day: and the man and his wife hid themselves
from the presence of the LORD God amongst the trees of
the garden. And the LORD God called unto the man, and 9
said unto him, Where art thou? And he said, I heard thy 10
voice in the garden, and I was afraid, because I was naked;
and I hid myself. And he said, Who told thee that thou 11
wast naked? Hast thou eaten of the tree, whereof I commanded thee that thou shouldest not eat? And the man 12
said, The woman whom thou gavest to be with me, she
gave me of the tree, and I did eat. And the LORD God 13
said unto the woman, What is this thou hast done? And
the woman said, The serpent beguiled me, and I did eat.
And the LORD God said unto the serpent, Because thou 14

---

6. The growing force of the temptation is well brought out by
the first three clauses. In the act of 'eating' the temptation
finally issued in the sin of disobedience. The common idea that
the forbidden fruit was an apple comes through the Latin.

7. the eyes...were opened: as promised by the serpent in *v.* 5.
But the result was first shame and then fear.

8. walking in the garden. Notice the *anthropomorphic*
language, God being represented as doing what an Eastern land-
owner would delight to do.

12. The woman whom thou gavest. Man's shame and fear
overcome his chivalry, and he tries to shift the blame. The fact
that the woman was the first to sin is emphasized also in Ecclus.
xxv. 24; 1 Tim. ii. 14.

hast done this, cursed art thou above all cattle, and above
every beast of the field; upon thy belly shalt thou go, and
15 dust shalt thou eat all the days of thy life: and I will put
enmity between thee and the woman, and between thy
seed and her seed: it shall bruise thy head, and thou shalt
16 bruise his heel. Unto the woman he said, I will greatly
multiply thy sorrow and thy conception; in sorrow thou
shalt bring forth children; and thy desire shall be to thy
17 husband, and he shall rule over thee. And unto Adam he
said, Because thou hast hearkened unto the voice of thy
wife, and hast eaten of the tree, of which I commanded
thee, saying, Thou shalt not eat of it: cursed is the ground
for thy sake; in toil shalt thou eat of it all the days of thy
18 life; thorns also and thistles shall it bring forth to thee;
19 and thou shalt eat the herb of the field; in the sweat of
thy face shalt thou eat bread, till thou return unto the
ground; for out of it wast thou taken: for dust thou art,
20 and unto dust shalt thou return. And the man called his
wife's name Eve; because she was the mother of all living.
21 And the LORD God made for Adam and for his wife coats
of skins, and clothed them.

---

14. upon thy belly shalt thou go: the serpent's characteristic mode of progress is represented as God's punishment. It
aptly suggests the insidious ways of evil.

15. it shall bruise thy head: the meaning of the verb is uncertain, 'bruise' agrees with the Latin Version. R.V. marg. 'lie
in wait for' is nearer to the Greek. The verse foretells the strife
between the power of evil and the higher nature of man, which
is to result in the victory of the latter. It cannot be said to refer
directly to our Lord's final triumph through the Cross, although
the age-long struggle culminated in that event.

16. The woman's punishment is the pain of child-bearing and
her subordinate position. There is no equality of the sexes in the
East, although in some Eastern countries it is developing in our
times.

17. The man's punishment is the sentence of toilsome labour
until death. Yet God's punishments often turn to blessings.

20. Eve: Hebrew Havvah, perhaps rather 'producing life.'

And the LORD God said, Behold, the man is become as 22
one of us, to know good and evil; and now, lest he put
forth his hand, and take also of the tree of life, and eat,
and live for ever: therefore the LORD God sent him forth 23
from the garden of Eden, to till the ground from whence
he was taken. So he drove out the man; and he placed 24
at the east of the garden of Eden the Cherubim, and the
flame of a sword which turned every way, to keep the way
of the tree of life.

iv. 1–16. *The story of Cain and Abel.*

And the man knew Eve his wife; and she conceived, 4
and bear Cain, and said, I have gotten a man with *the help
of* the LORD. And again she bare his brother Abel. And 2
Abel was a keeper of sheep, but Cain was a tiller of the
ground. And in process of time it came to pass, that Cain 3
brought of the fruit of the ground an offering unto the
LORD. And Abel, he also brought of the firstlings of his 4
flock and of the fat thereof. And the LORD had respect

---

22. is become as one of us. The words seem to imply
jealousy on the part of God, and we are reminded that we are
dealing with primitive religious ideas.

24. the Cherubim: regarded as angelic sentinels. As such
they have been compared with the winged figures which the
Assyrians depicted at the entrance of their temples. In Exod.
xxv. 18–20; 1 Kings vi. 23–28 they appear as figures over-
shadowing the mercy-seat above the ark. In Ps. xviii. 10 the
Cherub (sing.) seems to represent the storm-cloud depicted as
God's chariot.

iv. 1. I have gotten a man. The verb rendered *gotten* gives
a popular but unscientific etymology for Cain. We might say
I have gained.

with the help of the LORD: this is probably the best translation
of a very obscure passage.

2. Abel. The Hebrew word means 'breath,' perhaps referring
to Abel's short life. It may however rest upon a Babylonian
word meaning 'son.'

3. an offering: the first mention of sacrifice, which is represented in the earlier source J as a primitive instinct.

5 unto Abel and to his offering: but unto Cain and to his
  offering he had not respect. And Cain was very wroth,
6 and his countenance fell. And the LORD said unto Cain,
  Why art thou wroth? and why is thy countenance fallen?
7 If thou doest well, shalt thou not be accepted? and if thou
  doest not well, sin coucheth at the door: and unto thee
8 shall be his desire, and thou shalt rule over him. And
  Cain told Abel his brother. And it came to pass, when
  they were in the field, that Cain rose up against Abel his
9 brother, and slew him. And the LORD said unto Cain,
  Where is Abel thy brother? And he said, I know not: am
10 I my brother's keeper? And he said, What hast thou done?
  the voice of thy brother's blood crieth unto me from the
11 ground. And now cursed art thou from the ground, which

-----

5. he had not respect. The reason for this distinction is not
given, but it is sufficiently expressed in the words of 1 Sam. xvi. 7,
'the LORD looketh on the heart.' The Septuagint, or Greek
Version, does indeed suggest that Cain had committed some sort
of ritual error in his sacrifice.

7. shalt thou not be accepted? As so often in these early
narratives the terseness of the Hebrew renders it difficult to understand. R.V. marg. 'shall it (i.e. thy countenance) not be lifted
up?' is at least possible.

unto thee shall be his desire. Again obscure. R.V. makes
the thought very similar to that in ii. 16 where the word for
'desire' is the same The marg. 'unto thee is its desire, but thou
shouldest rule over it' pictures sin as a wild beast that seeks to
slay, but should be resisted.

8. told Abel his brother: lit. 'said to Abel.' We should
probably follow the ancient versions and read **said to Abel his
brother, Let us go into the field.**

9. am I my brother's keeper? The pertness of the words well
brings out the recklessness induced by sin. The world is only
slowly realizing that the answer to Cain's question is Yes.

10. the voice of thy brother's blood crieth. The blood is
personified as calling for vengeance: cf. Hebr. xii. 24, 'the blood
of sprinkling that speaketh better than that of Abel.' A similar
idea in Job xvi. 18. No emphasis can be laid on *the voice* of the
blood, as this is probably only an interjection 'Hark! thy brother's
blood crieth.' Cf. Isa. xl. 3.

hath opened her mouth to receive thy brother's blood from thy hand; when thou tillest the ground, it shall not hence- 12 forth yield unto thee her strength; a fugitive and a wanderer shalt thou be in the earth. And Cain said unto the 13 LORD, My punishment is greater than I can bear. Behold, 14 thou hast driven me out this day from the face of the ground; and from thy face shall I be hid; and I shall be a fugitive and a wanderer in the earth; and it shall come to pass, that whosoever findeth me shall slay me. And the 15 LORD said unto him, Therefore whosoever slayeth Cain, vengeance shall be taken on him sevenfold. And the LORD appointed a sign for Cain, lest any finding him should smite him.

And Cain went out from the presence of the LORD, and 16 dwelt in the land of Nod, on the east of Eden.

17–24. The beginning of civilization.

And Cain knew his wife; and she conceived, and bare 17 Enoch: and he builded a city, and called the name of the city, after the name of his son, Enoch. And unto Enoch 18 was born Irad: and Irad begat Mehujael: and Mehujael begat Methushael: and Methushael begat Lamech. And 19 Lamech took unto him two wives: the name of the one was Adah, and the name of the other Zillah. And Adah 20

---

15. sevenfold: cf. iv. 24.

appointed a sign. Possibly a mark on his forehead to shew that he was under Jehovah's protection. But this is not specified.

17. he builded a city. Obviously the literal truth of this must not be pressed. The writer is concerned to trace back the origins of institutions such as city life, music, and manufacture to the earliest times, and does not seem to realize that according to the narrative in Genesis there would be no one to inhabit the city, just as in *v.* 14 there would be no one to slay Cain.

19. Adah...Zillah: the names possibly mean Dawn and Dusk (lit. shadow).

bare Jabal: he was the father of such as dwell in tents
21 and *have* cattle. And his brother's name was Jubal: he
was the father of all such as handle the harp and pipe.
22 And Zillah, she also bare Tubal-cain, the forger of every
cutting instrument of brass and iron: and the sister of
23 Tubal-cain was Naamah. And Lamech said unto his wives:

> Adah and Zillah, hear my voice;
>
> Ye wives of Lamech, hearken unto my speech:
>
> For I have slain a man for wounding me,
>
> And a young man for bruising me:

24 > If Cain shall be avenged sevenfold,
>
> Truly Lamech seventy and sevenfold.

25 And Adam knew his wife again; and she bare a son,
and called his name Seth: For, *said she*, God hath appointed me another seed instead of Abel; for Cain slew
26 him. And to Seth, to him also there was born a son; and
he called his name Enosh: then began men to call upon
the name of the LORD.

v. *The line of men up to Noah.*

5 This is the book of the generations of Adam. In the
day that God created man, in the likeness of God made

---

20. such as dwell in tents. Nomad life seems to be regarded
as a later stage than city life.

22. brass and iron. The author rightly points out that the
beginning of the employment of metals marks a very important
stage in the progress of civilization. Lamech's song, evidently a
very old one, handed down through generations, is an outburst of
exultation at the thought that the invention of weapons of metal
had rendered him a dangerous foe to attack.

25. called his name Seth. This source gives but two verses
to Seth and his line, whereas in the next chapter the later source
(P) traces the line right down to Noah.

26. to call upon the name of the LORD: i.e. to worship God
under the name of Jehovah. In Exod. iii. 14 it is said that that
name was first revealed to Moses.

v. The stereotyped form of this chapter and the exact figures
given for each generation shew that we are dealing with the later

he him; male and female created he them; and blessed 2
them, and called their name Adam, in the day when they
were created. And Adam lived an hundred and thirty 3
years, and begat *a son* in his own likeness, after his image;
and called his name Seth: and the days of Adam after he 4
begat Seth were eight hundred years: and he begat sons
and daughters. And all the days that Adam lived were 5
nine hundred and thirty years: and he died.

And Seth lived an hundred and five years, and begat 6
Enosh: and Seth lived after he begat Enosh eight hundred 7
and seven years, and begat sons and daughters: and all 8
the days of Seth were nine hundred and twelve years: and
he died.

And Enosh lived ninety years, and begat Kenan: and 9, 10
Enosh lived after he begat Kenan eight hundred and fifteen
years, and begat sons and daughters: and all the days of 11
Enosh were nine hundred and five years: and he died.

And Kenan lived seventy years, and begat Mahalalel: and 12, 13
Kenan lived after he begat Mahalalel eight hundred and
forty years, and begat sons and daughters: and all the days 14
of Kenan were nine hundred and ten years: and he died.

And Mahalalel lived sixty and five years, and begat 15
Jared: and Mahalalel lived after he begat Jared eight 16
hundred and thirty years, and begat sons and daughters:
and all the days of Mahalalel were eight hundred ninety 17
and five years: and he died.

And Jared lived an hundred sixty and two years, and 18
begat Enoch: and Jared lived after he begat Enoch eight 19

Priestly source. Three figures are given for each patriarch
(*a*) the age at which his eldest son was born, (*b*) the remaining
years, (*c*) the total of his life. The great ages ascribed to the
patriarchs have always been a difficulty. There seems to be no
reason to imagine that primitive man was much more long-lived
than men of later ages, and it is best to say at once that the
figures are probably not historical.

20 hundred years, and begat sons and daughters: and all the
days of Jared were nine hundred sixty and two years:
and he died.

21 And Enoch lived sixty and five years, and begat Me-
22 thuselah: and Enoch walked with God after he begat
Methuselah three hundred years, and begat sons and
23 daughters: and all the days of Enoch were three hundred
24 sixty and five years: and Enoch walked with God: and
he was not; for God took him.

25 And Methuselah lived an hundred eighty and seven
26 years, and begat Lamech: and Methuselah lived after he
begat Lamech seven hundred eighty and two years, and
27 begat sons and daughters: and all the days of Methuselah
were nine hundred sixty and nine years: and he died.

28 And Lamech lived an hundred eighty and two years,
29 and begat a son: and he called his name Noah, saying,
This same shall comfort us for our work and for the toil
of our hands, because of the ground which the LORD hath
30 cursed. And Lamech lived after he begat Noah five hundred ninety and five years, and begat sons and daughters:
31 and all the days of Lamech were seven hundred seventy
and seven years: and he died.

---

24. Enoch walked with God. The same expression is used
of Noah in vi. 9. It denotes intimate communion.

he was not; for God took him: i.e. he did not die like other
men. There are three instances in the O.T. of a special passing
from life: Enoch, representing primitive man, Moses, representing the Law, and Elijah, representing the Prophets. It is to
be noted that Enoch's age is much less than that of the other
patriarchs. It *may* have some connection with the number of
days in the year. Enoch is an important figure in Jewish literature, and one of the most interesting of the Apocalyptic books is
called after him.

25. Methuselah is represented as the oldest of the patriarchs,
though Jared with 962 years comes very near him.

29. shall comfort us: another instance of false etymology.
Noah means 'rest,' and is quite different from the word meaning
'comfort.'

And Noah was five hundred years old : and Noah begat 32
Shem, Ham, and Japheth.

vi. 1–8. *The marriage of angels with the daughters of men.*

And it came to pass, when men began to multiply on 6
the face of the ground, and daughters were born unto
them, that the sons of God saw the daughters of men that 2
they were fair; and they took them wives of all that they
chose. And the LORD said, My spirit shall not strive with 3
man for ever, for that he also is flesh : yet shall his days be
an hundred and twenty years. The Nephilim were in the 4
earth in those days, and also after that, when the sons of
God came in unto the daughters of men, and they bare children to them : the same were the mighty men which were of
old, the men of renown. And the LORD saw that the wicked- 5
ness of man was great in the earth, and that every imagination of the thoughts of his heart was only evil continually.

---

vi. 1–8. The passage is difficult to understand. Some have
thought that the 'sons of God' are men of high rank, or perhaps
descendants of the line of Seth, and 'daughters of men' are
maidens of humble birth, and that the union between the two
classes tended to degeneration. But it seems better to understand
'sons of God' as angelic beings, and to see in the story a piece
of primitive folk-lore rather than actual history.

1. sons of God: not to be understood literally, but = 'supernatural beings.' Cf. such phrases as 'sons of men,' 'sons of Belial,'
'children of obedience.' For the expression cf. Job i. 6, ii. 1;
Ps. xxix. 1 (Heb.).

3. shall not strive: R.V. marg. shews that the verb is uncertain, and the following words 'for...flesh' obscure. R.V. text
implies that the frailty of man causes God to be long-suffering to
him : R.V. marg. that owing to man's feebleness and transgression
God must withdraw His spirit from him.

4. Nephilim: a race of giants mentioned also in Numb. xiii.
33. The fact that their name is connected with the Hebrew word
'to fall' gave rise to the idea that they were fallen angels.

6 And it repented the LORD that he had made man on the
7 earth, and it grieved him at his heart. And the LORD
said, I will destroy man whom I have created from the face
of the ground; both man, and beast, and creeping thing,
and fowl of the air; for it repenteth me that I have made
8 them. But Noah found grace in the eyes of the LORD.

vi. 9–ix. 17. *The story of the Flood.*

9   These are the generations of Noah. Noah was a righteous
man, *and* perfect in his generations: Noah walked with
10 God. And Noah begat three sons, Shem, Ham, and
11 Japheth. And the earth was corrupt before God, and the
12 earth was filled with violence. And God saw the earth,
and, behold, it was corrupt; for all flesh had corrupted
his way upon the earth.
13   And God said unto Noah, The end of all flesh is come
before me; for the earth is filled with violence through
them; and, behold, I will destroy them with the earth.
14 Make thee an ark of gopher wood; rooms shalt thou make
in he ark, and shalt pitch it within and without with pitch.
15 And this is how thou shalt make it: the length of the ark

---

6. it repented the LORD: cf. Exod. xxxii. 14; Judg. ii. 18;
1 Sam. xv. 11. Contrast 1 Sam. xv. 29. Men thought of God as
subject to human alterations of will and purpose.

9. perfect in his generations: cf. Ecclus. xliv. 17. So Job
is called 'perfect,' i.e. free from blemish, blameless.

walked with God: cf. v. 24.

14. an ark. The familiar word comes through the Latin
arca=box or chest. The Hebrew *tebah* is found outside this
passage only in Exod. ii. 3–5, of the ark in which Moses was laid.

gopher wood. The word is only found here, and the meaning
is uncertain. The Greek and Latin Versions have 'squared
beams.'

rooms: cf. nests, i.e. cubicles.

pitch: another word not found elsewhere in Hebrew in this
sense. The Babylonian story of the Flood uses the same root
with the same meaning, which tends to shew a direct connection
between the two accounts. Cf. Introd. p. 6.

three hundred cubits, the breadth of it fifty cubits, and the
height of it thirty cubits. A light shalt thou make to the 16
ark, and to a cubit shalt thou finish it upward; and the door
of the ark shalt thou set in the side thereof; with lower,
second, and third stories shalt thou make it. And I, be- 17
hold, I do bring the flood of waters upon the earth, to
destroy all flesh, wherein is the breath of life, from under
heaven; every thing that is in the earth shall die. But I 18
will establish my covenant with thee; and thou shalt come
into the ark, thou, and thy sons, and thy wife, and thy
sons' wives with thee. And of every living thing of all 19
flesh, two of every sort shalt thou bring into the ark, to
keep them alive with thee; they shall be male and female.
Of the fowl after their kind, and of the cattle after their 20
kind, of every creeping thing of the ground after its kind,
two of every sort shall come unto thee, to keep them alive.
And take thou unto thee of all food that is eaten, and 21
gather it to thee; and it shall be for food for thee, and for
them. Thus did Noah; according to all that God com- 22
manded him, so did he.

vii. *The story of the Flood continued (extracts from the
two accounts being woven together).*

And the LORD said unto Noah, Come thou and all thy 7
house into the ark; for thee have I seen righteous before

---

15. cubits. A cubit is the length from a man's elbow to the
tip of his fingers, about $1\frac{1}{2}$ ft.
16. A light: probably to be conceived of as a gap round the
sides of the ark just beneath the bottom of the roof, either a cubit
in height, or a cubit beneath the roof.
19. two of every sort. In the earlier document (J) there are
to be seven of the clean animals and two of the unclean. But P
regards these distinctions as part of the Law given at Sinai. So
vii. 8 is to be regarded as a harmonizing insertion of the compiler
of the narrative rather than an integral part of P.

2 me in this generation. Of every clean beast thou shalt
take to thee seven and seven, the male and his female;
and of the beasts that are not clean two, the male and his
3 female; of the fowl also of the air, seven and seven, male
and female: to keep seed alive upon the face of all the
4 earth. For yet seven days, and I will cause it to rain upon
the earth forty days and forty nights; and every living
thing that I have made will I destroy from off the face of
5 the ground. And Noah did according unto all that the
LORD commanded him.

6 And Noah was six hundred years old when the flood of
7 waters was upon the earth. And Noah went in, and his
sons, and his wife, and his sons' wives with him, into the
8 ark, because of the waters of the flood. Of clean beasts,
and of beasts that are not clean, and of fowls, and of every
9 thing that creepeth upon the ground, there went in two
and two unto Noah into the ark, male and female, as God
10 commanded Noah. And it came to pass after the seven
days, that the waters of the flood were upon the earth.
11 In the six hundredth year of Noah's life, in the second
month, on the seventeenth day of the month, on the same
day were all the fountains of the great deep broken up, and

---

vii. **2. every clean beast.** Clean and unclean creatures are
defined and specified in Levit. xi; Deut. xiv. 4-20.

4. forty days and forty nights. This is the duration of the
rain as given by J, cf. *vv.* 12, 17, viii. 6. In P the duration of
the Flood is 150 days, cf. vii. 24, viii. 3.

11. in the second month.... P gives a precise chronology.
The Flood begins on month 2 day 17: the ark rests on Ararat on
month 7 day 17. Next year on month 1 day 1 the Flood has still
further subsided, and on month 2 day 27 the earth is dry. The
duration of the Flood is therefore 12 months and 10 days. If the
space between the 17th day of the second and seventh month is
150 days, the month must be reckoned as 30 days.

the fountains of the great deep broken up. The Hebrews
imagined that there were vast reservoirs of water above the

the windows of heaven were opened. And the rain was 12
upon the earth forty days and forty nights. In the selfsame 13
day entered Noah, and Shem, and Ham, and Japheth, the
sons of Noah, and Noah's wife, and the three wives of his
sons with them, into the ark; they, and every beast after 14
its kind, and all the cattle after their kind, and every
creeping thing that creepeth upon the earth after its kind,
and every fowl after its kind, every bird of every sort. And 15
they went in unto Noah into the ark, two and two of all
flesh wherein is the breath of life. And they that went in, 16
went in male and female of all flesh, as God commanded
him: and the LORD shut him in. And the flood was forty 17
days upon the earth; and the waters increased, and bare
up the ark, and it was lift up above the earth. And the 18
waters prevailed, and increased greatly upon the earth;
and the ark went upon the face of the waters. And the 19
waters prevailed exceedingly upon the earth; and all the
high mountains that were under the whole heaven were
covered. Fifteen cubits upward did the waters prevail; 20
and the mountains were covered. And all flesh died that 21
moved upon the earth, both fowl, and cattle, and beast,
and every creeping thing that creepeth upon the earth,
and every man: all in whose nostrils was the breath of 22
the spirit of life, of all that was in the dry land, died.
And every living thing was destroyed which was upon the 23
face of the ground, both man, and cattle, and creeping
thing, and fowl of the heaven; and they were destroyed
from the earth: and Noah only was left, and they that
were with him in the ark. And the waters prevailed upon 24
the earth an hundred and fifty days.

---

sky and below the earth, both of which contributed to the
Flood.

20. Fifteen cubits upward: i.e. above the level of the high
mountains.

viii. 1-14. *The Flood subsides.*

8   And God remembered Noah, and every living thing, and all the cattle that were with him in the ark: and God made a wind to pass over the earth, and the waters
2 assuaged; the fountains also of the deep and the windows of heaven were stopped, and the rain from heaven was
3 restrained; and the waters returned from off the earth continually: and after the end of an hundred and fifty
4 days the waters decreased. And the ark rested in the seventh month, on the seventeenth day of the month, upon
5 the mountains of Ararat. And the waters decreased continually until the tenth month: in the tenth month, on the first day of the month, were the tops of the mountains
6 seen. And it came to pass at the end of forty days, that Noah opened the window of the ark which he had made:
7 and he sent forth a raven, and it went forth to and fro,
8 until the waters were dried up from off the earth. And he sent forth a dove from him, to see if the waters were
9 abated from off the face of the ground; but the dove found no rest for the sole of her foot, and she returned unto him to the ark, for the waters were on the face of the whole earth: and he put forth his hand, and took her, and brought
10 her in unto him into the ark. And he stayed yet other seven
11 days; and again he sent forth the dove out of the ark; and the dove came in to him at eventide; and, lo, in her mouth

---

viii. 4. the mountains of Ararat. Ararat was that part of Armenia which lies round Lake Van. It is an upland plateau with several mountains of which the highest is Mt Ararat (16,000 ft.). In the Babylonian account of the Flood the ship of Xisuthros rested on the mountain of Nizir.

7. a raven. The raven being a strong flier was able to maintain itself without returning to the ark: the dove when first sent out had to return. In the Babylonian account Xisuthros sends out successively a dove, a swallow and a raven, of which only the ast fails to return. Cf. Introd. p. 6.

an olive leaf pluckt off : so Noah knew that the waters were
abated from off the earth. And he stayed yet other seven 12
days ; and sent forth the dove ; and she returned not again
unto him any more. And it came to pass in the six hundred 13
and first year, in the first month, the first day of the month,
the waters were dried up from off the earth : and Noah
removed the covering of the ark, and looked, and, behold,
the face of the ground was dried. And in the second 14
month, on the seven and twentieth day of the month, was
the earth dry.

15–22. *The promise of the bow.*

And God spake unto Noah, saying, Go forth of the ark, ¹⁵₁₆
thou, and thy wife, and thy sons, and thy sons' wives with
thee. Bring forth with thee every living thing that is with 17
thee of all flesh, both fowl, and cattle, and every creeping
thing that creepeth upon the earth ; that they may breed
abundantly in the earth, and be fruitful, and multiply upon
the earth. And Noah went forth, and his sons, and his 18
wife, and his sons' wives with him : every beast, every 19
creeping thing, and every fowl, whatsoever moveth upon
the earth, after their families, went forth out of the ark.
And Noah builded an altar unto the LORD ; and took of 20
every clean beast, and of every clean fowl, and offered
burnt offerings on the altar. And the LORD smelled the 21
sweet savour ; and the LORD said in his heart, I will
not again curse the ground any more for man's sake, for
that the imagination of man's heart is evil from his youth ;
neither will I again smite any more every thing living, as

---

20. Noah builded an altar. Here we are back at the earlier
source J, for P recognizes no sacrifices till after the Law was
given at Sinai.

21. smelled the sweet savour. A relic of a primitive 'anthropomorphic' idea of God. The Babylonian account says that 'the
gods smelt the goodly savour of the sacrifice, and swarmed like
flies over the sacrifice.'

22 I have done. While the earth remaineth, seedtime and
harvest, and cold and heat, and summer and winter, and
day and night shall not cease.

ix. 1–17. *God's covenant with Noah.*

9 And God blessed Noah and his sons, and said unto them,
2 Be fruitful, and multiply, and replenish the earth. And the
fear of you and the dread of you shall be upon every beast
of the earth, and upon every fowl of the air ; with all wherewith the ground teemeth, and all the fishes of the sea, into
3 your hand are they delivered. Every moving thing that
liveth shall be food for you ; as the green herb have I given
4 you all. But flesh with the life thereof, *which is* the blood
5 thereof, shall ye not eat. And surely your blood, *the blood*
of your lives, will I require ; at the hand of every beast
will I require it : and at the hand of man, even at the hand
of every man's brother, will I require the life of man.
6 Whoso sheddeth man's blood, by man shall his blood be
7 shed : for in the image of God made he man. And you,

---

22. While the earth remaineth. As in the story of the Fall
(iii. 15), God's punishment is tempered with the promise of
blessing.

ix. 3. shall be food for you. According to P man becomes
carnivorous only after the Flood in accordance with God's permission. This permission is qualified by two restrictions (i) against
eating blood, (ii) against manslaughter.

4. with the life thereof. According to the Hebrew idea the
life was in the blood. Hence animals that were to be eaten had
to be killed according to special rules. This ordinance has per-
sisted to the present day, and Jews may only eat meat bought at
Kosher shops. Jewish butchers' shops may be distinguished by
the letters כשר (Kosher = ' proper ') on the windows.

6. Whoso sheddeth man's blood…: the *lex talionis* or law of
retaliation, a necessary ordinance in a community in which justice
is rough and there are no police. It appears as early as the time
of Cain (iv. 14). The nearest relative of the murdered man was
called the avenger of blood (Numb. xxxv. 19; Deut. xix. 6;
Josh. xx. 3). For cases of unintentional homicide the cities of
refuge were appointed.

be ye fruitful, and multiply; bring forth abundantly in the
earth, and multiply therein.

And God spake unto Noah, and to his sons with him, 8
saying, And I, behold, I establish my covenant with you, 9
and with your seed after you; and with every living creature 10
that is with you, the fowl, the cattle, and every beast of
the earth with you; of all that go out of the ark, even
every beast of the earth. And I will establish my covenant 11
with you; neither shall all flesh be cut off any more by the
waters of the flood; neither shall there any more be a
flood to destroy the earth. And God said, This is the 12
token of the covenant which I make between me and you
and every living creature that is with you, for perpetual
generations: I do set my bow in the cloud, and it shall be 13
for a token of a covenant between me and the earth. And 14
it shall come to pass, when I bring a cloud over the earth,
that the bow shall be seen in the cloud, and I will remember 15
my covenant, which is between me and you and every living
creature of all flesh; and the waters shall no more become
a flood to destroy all flesh. And the bow shall be in the 16
cloud; and I will look upon it, that I may remember the
everlasting covenant between God and every living creature of all flesh that is upon the earth. And God said unto 17

---

8. my covenant. The first occurrence of this word was in
vi. 18, but there it meant little more than a promise. In this
passage it has its full meaning, an agreement between God and
man. Sometimes it has a visible sign of its ratification: here it is
the rainbow, in xvii. 10 it is circumcision.

13. I do set. The Hebrew tense may be past, present, or
future. I *have*, *do*, or *will*, set. If the first meaning is taken it
implies that God now makes the rainbow, which has existed
before, the sign of the covenant. More probably the rainbow is
conceived of as coming now first into existence, and if so R.V.
text is right.

The rainbow being seen when the sun shines upon the rain
clouds is a fitting emblem of the promise that the earth should
never again be destroyed by water.

Noah, This is the token of the covenant which I have established between me and all flesh that is upon the earth,

18–29. *The trespass of Ham, the son of Noah.*

18 And the sons of Noah, that went forth of the ark, were Shem, and Ham, and Japheth: and Ham is the father of
19 Canaan. These three were the sons of Noah: and of these was the whole earth overspread.

20 And Noah began to be an husbandman, and planted a
21 vineyard: and he drank of the wine, and was drunken;
22 and he was uncovered within his tent. And Ham, the father of Canaan, saw the nakedness of his father, and
23 told his two brethren without. And Shem and Japheth took a garment, and laid it upon both their shoulders, and went backward, and covered the nakedness of their father; and their faces were backward, and they saw not their
24 father's nakedness. And Noah awoke from his wine, and
25 knew what his youngest son had done unto him. And he said,

Cursed be Canaan;

A servant of servants shall he be unto his brethren.

18-29. The narrative appears to have a double purpose: to trace agriculture and the growing of the vine back to Noah, and to account for the partial extermination of the Canaanites.

21. drank of the wine, and was drunken. He is represented as drinking in ignorance of the intoxicating effect of the wine.

22. Ham, the father of Canaan. There seems to be a little confusion, for while Ham is represented as committing the evil deed, it is Canaan on whom the curse is pronounced. It is interesting to find Canaan represented as a descendant of Ham, i.e. the African races.

25. The blessing or cursing pronounced by a father is represented as affecting the welfare of the son and his posterity. Cf. xxvii. 27 ff., 39 ff., xlviii. 20, xlix.

A servant of servants: i.e. the lowest servant. Cf. King of kings, and Lord of lords.

And he said,   26

      Blessed be the LORD, the God of Shem;
      And let Canaan be his servant.
      God enlarge Japheth,   27
      And let him dwell in the tents of Shem;
      And let Canaan be his servant.

And Noah lived after the flood three hundred and fifty 28
years. And all the days of Noah were nine hundred and 29
fifty years: and he died.

x. *The Table of Nations.*

Now these are the generations of the sons of Noah, **10**
Shem Ham and Japheth: and unto them were sons born
after the flood.

    The sons of Japheth; Gomer, and Magog, and Madai, 2
and Javan, and Tubal, and Meshech, and Tiras. And the 3
sons of Gomer; Ashkenaz, and Riphath, and Togarmah.

---

27. God enlarge Japheth. There is in Hebrew a play on the
words 'enlarge' and 'Japheth' which are very similar. So in
xxi. 6 there is a play on Isaac, and in xxvii. 36 on Jacob.

let him dwell in the tents of Shem: i.e. let them associate on
equal terms together.

The blessing obviously refers to the races which were sprung
from the sons of Noah. It is not certain who are the descendants
of Japheth who are to dwell in the tents of Shem. Some have
thought that the Philistines are meant.

x. The chapter though apparently a rather dull catalogue of
names is really full of interest, as giving the Hebrew idea of the
relationship of peoples and tribes to one another. They are divided into three main families corresponding with the three sons
of Noah. The names cannot by any means all be identified, but
we can see the general idea in the mind of the compiler.

2. sons of Japheth. Gomer probably stands for Cimmerians
in S. Russia, **Magog** for Scythians, **Madai** for Medes, **Javan** for
Greeks (Ionians). **Tubal** and **Meshech** (Ps. cxx. 5) were tribes
in N.E. Asia Minor: **Tiras** is not certainly identified.

3. Ashkenaz: cf. Jer. li. 27: perhaps = Armenia. Modern
Jews are divided into two sections, Ashkenazim and Sephardim,
corresponding to German and Spanish.

4 And the sons of Javan; Elishah, and Tarshish, Kittim,
5 and Dodanim. Of these were the isles of the nations
divided in their lands, every one after his tongue; after
their families, in their nations.

6   And the sons of Ham; Cush, and Mizraim, and Put,
7 and Canaan. And the sons of Cush; Seba, and Havilah,
and Sabtah, and Raamah, and Sabteca: and the sons of
8 Raamah; Sheba, and Dedan. And Cush begat Nimrod:
9 he began to be a mighty one in the earth. He was a
mighty hunter before the LORD: wherefore it is said, Like
10 Nimrod a mighty hunter before the LORD. And the beginning of his kingdom was Babel, and Erech, and Accad,
11 and Calneh, in the land of Shinar. Out of that land he
went forth into Assyria, and builded Nineveh, and Reho-
12 both-Ir, and Calah, and Resen between Nineveh and
13 Calah (the same is the great city). And Mizraim begat
14 Ludim, and Anamim, and Lehabim, and Naphtuhim, and
Pathrusim, and Casluhim (whence went forth the Philistines), and Caphtorim.

---

4. sons of Javan: i.e. Greek colonies. **Elishah** is uncertain,
Tarshish (Ps. lxxii. 10; Isa. lx. 9; Jonah i. 3 etc.) is probably Tar-
tessus, a sea-town in Spain, **Kittim** represents the people of Cyprus,
and **Dodanim** (or rather **Rodanim**, 1 Chr. i. 7) the people of
Rhodes.

6. sons of Ham. **Cush** stands for Ethiopia, **Mizraim** is Egypt,
Put probably Libya, and **Canaan**, Palestine and Phœnicia.

8. Nimrod: apparently the founder of the Babylonian and
Assyrian Empires. He has been identified with Gilgamesh the
hero of the famous Babylonian Epic.

9. a mighty hunter. The kings of Babylon and Assyria delight to display their prowess in hunting in reliefs cut out of stone.

10. Babel is of course Babylon, **Erech** the ancient Uruk of
which Gilgamesh was ruler, **Accad** a district, and perhaps a city,
in N. Babylonia. **Shinar** is the ancient name of Babylonia.

11. Nineveh: on the Tigris opposite to Mosul. It reached its
greatest prosperity under Sennacherib (704–682 B.C.) and was
destroyed in 606 B.C.

14. Pathrusim: the inhabitants of Upper (i.e. Southern)
Egypt. Cf. Isa. xi. 11; Jer. xliv, 1, 15.

Caphtorim: the people of Crete, Deut. ii. 23; Amos ix. 7. As

And Canaan begat Zidon his firstborn, and Heth ; and $^{15}_{16}$
the Jebusite, and the Amorite, and the Girgashite ; and 17
the Hivite, and the Arkite, and the Sinite ; and the Arvad- 18
ite, and the Zemarite, and the Hamathite: and afterward
were the families of the Canaanite spread abroad. And 19
the border of the Canaanite was from Zidon, as thou goest
toward Gerar, unto Gaza; as thou goest toward Sodom
and Gomorrah and Admah and Zeboiim, unto Lasha.
These are the sons of Ham, after their families, after their 20
tongues, in their lands, in their nations.

And unto Shem, the father of all the children of Eber, 21
the elder brother of Japheth, to him also were children
born. The sons of Shem; Elam, and Asshur, and Arpach- 22
shad, and Lud, and Aram. And the sons of Aram ; Uz, 23

---

the Philistines are said to have come from Caphtor it has been
thought that the note 'whence…Philistines' should come at the
end of the verse.

15. Zidon his firstborn. Zidon or Sidon was the most ancient
city of Phœnicia, though it was overshadowed later by Tyre.

Heth (xxiii. 3 etc.): refers to the Hittites, whose empire
stretched at one time as far as the Mediterranean, though it is
very doubtful whether they had any affinity with the Phœnicians.

16. Jebusite: the original inhabitants of Jerusalem, Judg. i. 21;
2 Sam. v. 6.

Amorite: sometimes used to include generally the original inhabitants of Palestine, cf. Amos ii. 9: sometimes more specially
of the people ruled over by Sihon, Numb. xxi. 13.

19. Admah and Zeboiim: two cities destroyed with Sodom
and Gomorrah. Deut. xxix. 23; Hos. xi. 8.

21. children of Eber. Eber is regarded as the ancestor of the
Hebrews, the root being the same.

22. sons of Shem. Elam was a great empire in very early
times, with its capital at Susa. **Asshur** is the Assyrians, with
their capital at Nineveh. **Lud** refers to the Lydians, and **Aram**
includes all the various Syrian tribes. **Arpachshad** is not satis-
factorily explained, but the last part of the name may contain the
word Chasdim or Chaldæans.

23. Uz: the birthplace of Job; perhaps just north of Edom.
The names that follow are either uncertain or comparatively
unimportant.

24 and Hul, and Gether, and Mash. And Arpachshad begat
25 Shelah; and Shelah begat Eber. And unto Eber were
born two sons: the name of the one was Peleg; for in his
days was the earth divided; and his brother's name was
26 Joktan. And Joktan begat Almodad, and Sheleph, and
27 Hazarmaveth, and Jerah; and Hadoram, and Uzal, and
²⁸₂₉ Diklah; and Obal, and Abimael, and Sheba; and Ophir,
and Havilah, and Jobab: all these were the sons of Joktan.
30 And their dwelling was from Mesha, as thou goest toward
31 Sephar, the mountain of the east. These are the sons of
Shem, after their families, after their tongues, in their
lands, after their nations.

32   These are the families of the sons of Noah, after their
generations, in their nations: and of these were the nations
divided in the earth after the flood.

xi. 1–9. *The story of the Tower of Babel.*

11   And the whole earth was of one language and of one
2 speech. And it came to pass, as they journeyed east, that
they found a plain in the land of Shinar; and they dwelt
3 there. And they said one to another, Go to, let us make
brick, and burn them throughly. And they had brick for
4 stone, and slime had they for mortar. And they said, Go
to, let us build us a city, and a tower, whose top *may reach*

---

xi. 1–9. The story gives an explanation of the diversities of
languages in the world. They are represented as God's punishment
for man's overweening pride caused by the spread of civilization.
    1. one language. The Jews imagined that their own language
was the primitive one.
    2. a plain: the word means a cleft or valley.
    3. slime: i.e. bitumen. Obviously the writer is more familiar
with stone buildings, but there is little or no stone in Babylonia.
    4. a tower. Lofty towers were a feature of ancient Babylonia,
and they may have suggested the origin of this legend. One of
the most celebrated is the Birs Nimroud which is described in
Layard's *Nineveh and Babylon*, pp. 495 ff.

unto heaven, and let us make us a name; lest we be scattered abroad upon the face of the whole earth. And the 5 LORD came down to see the city and the tower, which the children of men builded. And the LORD said, Behold, 6 they are one people, and they have all one language; and this is what they begin to do: and now nothing will be withholden from them, which they purpose to do. Go to, 7 let us go down, and there confound their language, that they may not understand one another's speech. So the 8 LORD scattered them abroad from thence upon the face of all the earth: and they left off to build the city. There- 9 fore was the name of it called Babel; because the LORD did there confound the language of all the earth: and from thence did the LORD scatter them abroad upon the face of all the earth.

10–26. *The genealogy of Shem.*

These are the generations of Shem. Shem was an hun- 10 dred years old, and begat Arpachshad two years after the flood: and Shem lived after he begat Arpachshad five 11 hundred years, and begat sons and daughters.

And Arpachshad lived five and thirty years, and begat 12

---

4 lest we be scattered. The tower was to be a rallying point, and a visible token of union.

5. the LORD came down. To the primitive mind of the author it was necessary for God to come down before He could examine the tower.

7. let us go down: for the plural see note on i. 26.

9. Babel: another instance of popular etymology. The word suggested to the Hebrew a root meaning 'confuse,' but more probably it is a compound word meaning 'God's gate.'

10–26. Obviously we return to the precise and regular style of the later source (P). The object of the section is to put Abraham into his chronological setting. Nine generations intervene between Shem and Terah the father of Abraham. The number of years in this period is 390 according to the Hebrew Massoretic text, and 1170 according to the LXX.

13 Shelah : and Arpachshad lived after he begat Shelah four
hundred and three years, and begat sons and daughters.

14
15 And Shelah lived thirty years, and begat Eber : and
Shelah lived after he begat Eber four hundred and three
years, and begat sons and daughters.

16 And Eber lived four and thirty years, and begat Peleg:
17 and Eber lived after he begat Peleg four hundred and
thirty years, and begat sons and daughters.

18
19 And Peleg lived thirty years, and begat Reu: and Peleg
lived after he begat Reu two hundred and nine years, and
begat sons and daughters.

20 And Reu lived two and thirty years, and begat Serug :
21 and Reu lived after he begat Serug two hundred and seven
years, and begat sons and daughters.

22
2 And Serug lived thirty years, and begat Nahor: and
Serug lived after he begat Nahor two hundred years, and
begat sons and daughters.

24 And Nahor lived nine and twenty years, and begat
25 Terah : and Nahor lived after he begat Terah an hundred
and nineteen years, and begat sons and daughters.

26 And Terah lived seventy years, and begat Abram, Nahor, and Haran.

27–32. *The sons of Terah.*

27 Now these are the generations of Terah. Terah begat
28 Abram, Nahor, and Haran ; and Haran begat Lot. And
Haran died in the presence of his father Terah in the land
29 of his nativity, in Ur of the Chaldees. And Abram and
Nahor took them wives : the name of Abram's wife was
Sarai; and the name of Nahor's wife, Milcah, the daughter
of Haran, the father of Milcah, and the father of Iscah.

---

28. Haran died. This explains why Lot is found with Abram.
29. Nahor's wife. Nahor is represented as marrying his niece,
and Abram his half-sister. But possibly we are to understand
rather tribal than family relationships.

And Sarai was barren; she had no child. And Terah took 30 31
Abram his son, and Lot the son of Haran, his son's son,
and Sarai his daughter in law, his son Abram's wife; and
they went forth with them from Ur of the Chaldees, to go
into the land of Canaan; and they came unto Haran, and
dwelt there. And the days of Terah were two hundred 32
and five years: and Terah died in Haran.

xii. 1–9. *Abram's migration to Canaan.*

Now the LORD said unto Abram, Get thee out of thy 12
country, and from thy kindred, and from thy father's house,
unto the land that I will shew thee: and I will make of 2
thee a great nation, and I will bless thee, and make thy
name great; and be thou a blessing: and I will bless 3
them that bless thee; and him that curseth thee will I
curse: and in thee shall all the families of the earth be
blessed. So Abram went, as the LORD had spoken unto 4
him; and Lot went with him: and Abram was seventy
and five years old when he departed out of Haran. And 5

---

31. from Ur of the Chaldees: a very ancient city, the site of
which has been identified at a spot near the Euphrates about
125 miles from its present mouth. It was dedicated to the
moon-god.

Haran: later Carrhae, the scene of the defeat of Crassus in
53 B.C. It lies 550 miles N.W. of Ur. The word in Assyrian
means 'road.' Like Ur it was a centre of the worship of the moon.

xii. 1–9. This chapter may be regarded as the beginning of actual
Biblical history, as distinguished from historical folk-lore. God
singles out Abram as the recipient of His promise, on the con
dition that he obeys His command. So by his obedience Abram
becomes the 'father of the faithful.'

1. unto the land. In xi. 31 it was said that Terah and his
family set out from Ur to go into the land of Canaan, but they
had got no further than Haran.

3. in thee...be blessed. The words may mean (*a*) that
Abram's descendants will be a source of blessing to all the
world, (*b*) that they should be a type or illustration of a people
blessed by God. 'In thee...shall all the families of the earth bless
themselves,' i.e. they shall use thee...as a type of blessing.

Abram took Sarai his wife, and Lot his brother's son, and
all their substance that they had gathered, and the souls
that they had gotten in Haran; and they went forth to go
into the land of Canaan; and into the land of Canaan
6 they came. And Abram passed through the land unto the
place of Shechem, unto the oak of Moreh. And the Ca-
7 naanite was then in the land. And the LORD appeared
unto Abram, and said, Unto thy seed will I give this
land: and there builded he an altar unto the LORD, who
8 appeared unto him. And he removed from thence unto
the mountain on the east of Beth-el, and pitched his tent,
having Beth-el on the west, and Ai on the east: and there
he builded an altar unto the LORD, and called upon the
9 name of the LORD. And Abram journeyed, going on still
toward the South.

xii. 10–xiii. 2. *Abram goes down to Egypt.*

10   And there was a famine in the land: and Abram went
down into Egypt to sojourn there; for the famine was sore
11 in the land. And it came to pass, when he was come near
to enter into Egypt, that he said unto Sarai his wife, Behold now, I know that thou art a fair woman to look upon:

---

6. unto the place of Shechem. An ancient sanctuary in the
middle of the land: modern Nablus. Its holiness was apparently
originally derived from a sacred oak from which oracles were
derived, as from the oaks of Dodona in ancient Greece. **Moreh**
may mean the 'teacher' or 'director.' In the ancient Canaanite
nature-religion large trees were regarded as the abodes of a god.

7. the LORD appeared: making Shechem a holy place for the
Israelites.

8. Beth-el. In xxviii. 12 the original name of the place is said to
have been Luz, and the name Beth-el to have been given by Jacob.

10. went down into Egypt. Egypt was usually the place of
refuge from famine for the people of Palestine, for, not being
dependent on the rainfall, its crops were more regular. A journey
from Palestine to Egypt is regularly spoken of as 'going down'
and the reverse journey as 'coming up.'

11. a fair woman. This narrative obviously represents Sarai

and it shall come to pass, when the Egyptians shall see 12
thee, that they shall say, This is his wife: and they will
kill me, but they will save thee alive. Say, I pray thee, 13
thou art my sister: that it may be well with me for thy
sake, and that my soul may live because of thee. And it 14
came to pass, that, when Abram was come into Egypt,
the Egyptians beheld the woman that she was very fair.
And the princes of Pharaoh saw her, and praised her to 15
Pharaoh: and the woman was taken into Pharaoh's house.
And he entreated Abram well for her sake: and he had 16
sheep, and oxen, and he-asses, and menservants, and
maidservants, and she-asses, and camels. And the LORD 17
plagued Pharaoh and his house with great plagues because
of Sarai Abram's wife. And Pharaoh called Abram, and 18
said, What is this that thou hast done unto me? why didst
thou not tell me that she was thy wife? Why saidst thou, 19
She is my sister? so that I took her to be my wife: now
therefore behold thy wife, take her, and go thy way. And 20
Pharaoh gave men charge concerning him: and they
brought him on the way, and his wife, and all that
he had.

---

as young, though according to the other source she must have
been at least 65 (cf. xii. 4 with xvii. 17).

15. Pharaoh: a title applied to all kings of Egypt. It is said
to mean Great House. Cf. 'Sublime Porte' as referring to the
court and government of Turkey.

16. entreated: an archaism, or old-world expression, for
'treated.' Cf. Exod. v. 22; 1 Thess. ii. 2 and (in A.V.) Lk. xx.
11; Acts xxvii. 3.

17. the LORD plagued Pharaoh. Pharaoh was punished because he had committed a sin although unwittingly. This rather
mechanical conception of punishment following 'sin' is characteristic of early religion. It is not implied that Abram had done
wrong, although to our minds he was the worse offender. However Pharaoh has him deported from the land.

20. they brought him on the way. A mark of special honour
to atone for Pharaoh's treatment of Sarai.

xiii. *Abram returns to Canaan and separates from Lot.*

13 And Abram went up out of Egypt, he, and his wife, and
2 all that he had, and Lot with him, into the South. And
3 Abram was very rich in cattle, in silver, and in gold. And
he went on his journeys from the South even to Beth-el,
unto the place where his tent had been at the beginning,
4 between Beth-el and Ai; unto the place of the altar, which
he had made there at the first: and there Abram called
5 on the name of the LORD. And Lot also, which went with
6 Abram, had flocks, and herds, and tents. And the land
was not able to bear them, that they might dwell together:
for their substance was great, so that they could not dwell
7 together. And there was a strife between the herdmen of
Abram's cattle and the herdmen of Lot's cattle: and the
Canaanite and the Perizzite dwelled then in the land.
8 And Abram said unto Lot, Let there be no strife, I pray
thee, between me and thee, and between my herdmen and
9 thy herdmen; for we are brethren. Is not the whole land
before thee? separate thyself, I pray thee, from me: if
thou wilt take the left hand, then I will go to the right;
or if *thou take* the right hand, then I will go to the left.
10 And Lot lifted up his eyes, and beheld all the Plain of

---

xiii. 1. into the South: lit. the *Negeb*, a geographical term
denoting the somewhat desolate land on the southern frontier of
Palestine.

2. in silver, and in gold: apparently he had realized many of
the possessions he had had in Egypt.

4. called on the name of the LORD: a common phrase for
'performed an act of worship.' Cf. iv. 26, xii. 8, xxi. 33 etc.

7. the Perizzite: often named with the Canaanites. The name
is supposed to mean 'village dwellers.'

8. we are brethren: i.e. kinsmen. They were actually uncle
and nephew.

9. It is a mark of special generosity that Abram offers Lot the
first choice.

10. the Plain of Jordan. Another geographical term, strictly
the *circle* of Jordan. The writer pictured the space now covered
by the Dead Sea as a smiling landscape.

Jordan, that it was well watered every where, before the
LORD destroyed Sodom and Gomorrah, like the garden
of the LORD, like the land of Egypt, as thou goest unto
Zoar. So Lot chose him all the Plain of Jordan; and Lot 11
journeyed east: and they separated themselves the one
from the other. Abram dwelled in the land of Canaan, 12
and Lot dwelled in the cities of the Plain, and moved his
tent as far as Sodom. Now the men of Sodom were wicked 13
and sinners against the LORD exceedingly. And the LORD 14
said unto Abram, after that Lot was separated from him,
Lift up now thine eyes, and look from the place where
thou art, northward and southward and eastward and
westward: for all the land which thou seest, to thee will 15
I give it, and to thy seed for ever. And I will make thy 16
seed as the dust of the earth: so that if a man can number
the dust of the earth, then shall thy seed also be numbered.
Arise, walk through the land in the length of it and in the 17
breadth of it; for unto thee will I give it. And Abram 18
moved his tent, and came and dwelt by the oaks of Mamre,

---

10. well watered. Besides the Jordan and the Arnon many
smaller streams empty themselves into the Dead Sea on either side.

unto Zoar: the site of Zoar is not certain. From Deut. xxxiv. 3
it would appear to be at the north end of the Dead Sea. Some
versions read Zoan, which is in Egypt.

11. Lot chose. It is implied that Lot's choice was a worldly
one, and that he should have avoided all association with the
inhabitants of the cities of the Plain.

14. Lift up now thine eyes. Abram seemed to have the worse
part of the land assigned to him, but he is encouraged by God's
renewed blessing.

16. as the dust of the earth: cf. xxviii. 14; 2 Chr. i. 9.
Other common figures for an innumerable multitude are 'the
sand of the sea' and 'the stars of heaven.'

18. the oaks of Mamre. Sacred trees such as the oak of Moreh,
xii. 6. Possibly the word should be in the sing. (as in LXX),
both here and in xviii. 1 referring to a well-known tree. Hebron
has for many centuries been famous for its ancient oaks or
terebinths. One which was known as Abraham's oak was split
by lightning in 1868.

which are in Hebron, and built there an altar unto the
LORD.

xiv. *The battle of the kings and the story of Melchizedek.*

14 And it came to pass in the days of Amraphel king of
Shinar, Arioch king of Ellasar, Chedorlaomer king of
2 Elam, and Tidal king of Goiim, that they made war with
Bera king of Sodom, and with Birsha king of Gomorrah,
Shinab king of Admah, and Shemeber king of Zeboiim,
3 and the king of Bela (the same is Zoar). All these joined
together in the vale of Siddim (the same is the Salt Sea).
4 Twelve years they served Chedorlaomer, and in the thir-
5 teenth year they rebelled. And in the fourteenth year came
Chedorlaomer, and the kings that were with him, and
smote the Rephaim in Ashteroth-karnaim, and the Zuzim

Hebron: still an important place, and a holy city of the Moslems who call it after Abraham *El Khalil* the 'Friend' (of God).

xiv. This chapter appears to stand by itself and to be derived
from a special source.

1. Amraphel king of Shinar. It is generally supposed that
he is to be identified with Hammurabi, king of Babylon, whose
date is somewhere round about 2000 B.C. He was a great warrior
and statesman, and is chiefly famous for his Code of Laws which
was discovered in 1902 at Susa, written in some 49 columns on a
block of diorite. These laws, which presuppose an advanced state
of civilization, are in many respects parallel to the Mosaic Law.

Arioch king of Ellasar. An ancient inscription speaks of
'Eriaku king of Larsa' who may be identified with this Arioch.

Chedorlaomer king of Elam. Elam was an important country
north of the Persian Gulf, with its capital at Susa. Some late
tablets in the British Museum tell how a king of Elam with a
name like Chedorlaomer invaded Babylonia and plundered its
cities and temples. If this is historical it may have happened
during the twelve years mentioned in *v.* 4, for after this Chedorlaomer and not Amraphel is the leader.

Tidal king of Goiim. Goiim in Hebrew means 'nations,' but
it may represent a name sounding somewhat similar. Tidal is
not known.

2. The five cities of the Plain are spoken of in Wisdom x. 6
as the Pentapolis.

5. Rephaim...Zuzim...Emim...Horites. The four peoples are

in Ham, and the Emim in Shaveh-kiriathaim, and the 6
Horites in their mount Seir, unto El-paran, which is by
the wilderness. And they returned, and came to En- 7
mishpat (the same is Kadesh), and smote all the country of
the Amalekites, and also the Amorites, that dwelt in Hazazon-tamar. And there went out the king of Sodom, and 8
the king of Gomorrah, and the king of Admah, and the
king of Zeboiim, and the king of Bela (the same is Zoar);
and they set the battle in array against them in the vale
of Siddim ; against Chedorlaomer king of Elam, and Tidal 9
king of Goiim, and Amraphel king of Shinar, and Arioch
king of Ellasar ; four kings against the five. Now the vale 10
of Siddim was full of slime pits ; and the kings of Sodom
and Gomorrah fled, and they fell there, and they that re-
mained fled to the mountain. And they took all the 11
goods of Sodom and Gomorrah, and all their victuals, and
went their way. And they took Lot, Abram's brother's 12
son, who dwelt in Sodom, and his goods, and departed.
And there came one that had escaped, and told Abram the 13

mentioned together again in Deut. ii. 10–12, 20 as original inhabitants of Palestine. The Zuzim are there called Zamzummim.

Ashteroth-karnaim: lit. Ashtaroth of the double horn. The
town seems to have stood in a very strong position on the river
Yarmuk. It is not mentioned again in the O.T., but it was the
scene of much fighting in the time of the Maccabees.

7. En-mishpat: lit. the spring of judgment, cf. En-gedi,
En-rogel. Apparently it was a sacred spring (hence the other
name Kadesh = sacred) at which oracles were obtained. Kadesh or
Kadesh-barnea lies about 50 miles S. of Beer-sheba. Cf. Numb.
xx. 1 ff. ; Deut. i. 46.

Amalekites: a Bedouin tribe against which Saul won a victory
(1 Sam. xv. Cf. also 2 Sam. i. 8, 13).

Hazazon-tamar: lit. the felling of the palm tree, identified in
2 Chr. xx. 2 with En-gedi.

10. slime pits or **bitumen wells**. Possibly like the great as-
phalt lake in Trinidad.

to the mountain: i.e. the mountains of Moab east of the Dead
Sea, cf. xix. 17.

13. Abram the Hebrew. The word Hebrew, which is here

Hebrew: now he dwelt by the oaks of Mamre the Amorite, brother of Eshcol, and brother of Aner; and these
14 were confederate with Abram. And when Abram heard that his brother was taken captive, he led forth his trained men, born in his house, three hundred and eighteen, and
15 pursued as far as Dan. And he divided himself against them by night, he and his servants, and smote them, and pursued them unto Hobah, which is on the left hand of
16 Damascus. And he brought back all the goods, and also brought again his brother Lot, and his goods, and the
17 women also, and the people. And the king of Sodom went out to meet him, after his return from the slaughter of Chedorlaomer and the kings that were with him, at the
18 vale of Shaveh (the same is the King's Vale). And Melchizedek king of Salem brought forth bread and wine:

---

used for the first time, means either 'the descendant of Eber' (x. 24) or more probably 'the man from beyond the river' (Euphrates).

14. his brother: see v. 16. Cf. xiii. 8.

three hundred and eighteen. The precision of the number is curious, and Jewish and early Christian writers found in it a mystical meaning. Abram is represented as a great sheikh or petty king with a considerable armed force at his disposal.

as far as Dan. Dan lay in the far north, but its mention here is an anachronism, as the name is first given in the time of Joshua. Cf. Josh. xix. 47; Judg. xviii. 29.

15. divided himself: probably into three bands of 106 each. Cf. the strategy of Gideon (Judg. vii. 20-22) and Saul (1 Sam. xi. 11).

unto Hobah: some 50 miles N. of Damascus. The pursuit was therefore a very long one. In reckoning the points of the compass the Hebrews always faced eastward. Hence the left is N., the right S., and behind W.

18. Melchizedek king of Salem. The name Melchizedek means, as the author of the Ep. to the Hebrews points out (vii. 2), king of righteousness, and Salem which probably stands for Jerusalem is very like the word for 'peace.' But Zedek appears to have been a Canaanite god, so Melchizedek might mean Zedek is my king, just as another king of Jerusalem is called Adonizedek (Josh. x. 1) which may mean 'Zedek is my lord.'

bread and wine: i.e. as refreshment for the men. So Ziba sent refreshment to David's men, 2 Sam. xvi. 1, 2.

and he was priest of God Most High. And he blessed 19
him, and said, Blessed be Abram of God Most High,
possessor of heaven and earth: and blessed be God Most 20
High, which hath delivered thine enemies into thy hand.
And he gave him a tenth of all. And the king of Sodom said 21
unto Abram, Give me the persons, and take the goods to
thyself. And Abram said to the king of Sodom, I have lift 22
up mine hand unto the LORD, God Most High, possessor
of heaven and earth, that I will not take a thread nor a 23
shoelatchet nor aught that is thine, lest thou shouldest say,
I have made Abram rich: save only that which the young 24
men have eaten, and the portion of the men which went
with me; Aner, Eshcol, and Mamre, let them take their
portion.

xv. *God promises to Abram a son and wide possessions,*
   and ratifies His promise by a solemn covenant.

After these things the word of the LORD came unto 15
Abram in a vision, saying, Fear not, Abram: I am thy
shield, *and* thy exceeding great reward. And Abram said, 2

---

18. priest of God Most High. Melchizedek combined the offices
of king and priest. The Hebrew writer regards him as priest of
the true God, though some modern scholars have maintained that
El Elyon (rendered God Most High) was the name of a Canaanite
god. For his priesthood cf. Ps. cx. 4. It is characteristic of the
writer of the Ep. to the Hebrews to see in Melchizedek a supreme
representative of primitive pre-Israelite religion and a type of
Christ.

19. possessor: rather 'author' or 'maker' (R.V. marg.).

20. he gave him: i.e. Abram gave Melchizedek.

a tenth of all: i.e. the spoil. It was customary in very early
times to give to the priest a tenth of the produce of the land.
Here Abram is represented as recognizing the duty which was
enjoined on the Israelites in later days.

xv. 1. thy shield: a common figure, cf. 2 Sam. xxii. 3;
Ps. iii. 3, xxviii. 7, lxxxiv. 9.

thy exceeding great reward. It is possible that God might
be spoken of as the reward rather than the rewarder, but R.V.
marg., *thy reward shall be exceeding great,* is more probable.

O Lord GOD, what wilt thou give me, seeing I go childless,
and he that shall be possessor of my house is Dammesek
3 Eliezer? And Abram said, Behold, to me thou hast given
no seed: and, lo, one born in my house is mine heir.
4 And, behold, the word of the LORD came unto him, saying,
This man shall not be thine heir; but he that shall come
5 forth out of thine own bowels shall be thine heir. And he
brought him forth abroad, and said, Look now toward
heaven, and tell the stars, if thou be able to tell them: and
6 he said unto him, So shall thy seed be. And he believed
in the LORD; and he counted it to him for righteousness.
7 And he said unto him, I am the LORD that brought thee
out of Ur of the Chaldees, to give thee this land to in-
8 herit it. And he said, O Lord GOD, whereby shall I know
9 that I shall inherit it? And he said unto him, Take me
an heifer of three years old, and a she-goat of three years

---

2. possessor of my house: i.e. my heir in default of children.
is Dammesek Eliezer. The words form an unsolved problem.
Dammesek is the Hebrew name for Damascus, but there seems
no reason for introducing Damascus here. Possibly Dammesek
represents an Aramaic gloss on 'possessor of my house.' Perhaps
it might be rendered *steward*. Obviously the man's name was
Eliezer, and an ingenious Jewish writer has noticed that the
numerical value of the letters of Eliezer is 318, the number of
Abram's trained servants (xiv. 14).

5. to tell them: i.e. to count them. Cf. Ps. xxii. 17, xlviii. 12.
To the Hebrew the stars were innumerable (cf. xxii. 17, xxvi. 4 etc.),
and modern telescopes have only served to emphasize this
thought.

6. The verse on which St Paul built up his great argument in
Romans iv. ff.

9. Take me an heifer. The ritual described is a very ancient
one. Certain animals were slain, and their carcases divided into
two parts, and then the parties to the contract walked between
the two parts, to signify that if they violated the contract they
acknowledged themselves worthy to be slain as the animals were.
Here God is depicted as sanctioning, or possibly inaugurating,
this form of ritual, and the smoking furnace and flaming torch
(*v.* 17) represent Him. For the ritual in later times cf. Jer.
xxxiv. 18.

old, and a ram of three years old, and a turtledove, and a
young pigeon. And he took him all these, and divided 10
them in the midst, and laid each half over against the
other : but the birds divided he not. And the birds of prey 11
came down upon the carcases, and Abram drove them
away. And when the sun was going down, a deep sleep 12
fell upon Abram ; and, lo, an horror of great darkness fell
upon him. And he said unto Abram, Know of a surety 13
that thy seed shall be a stranger in a land that is not
theirs, and shall serve them ; and they shall afflict them
four hundred years ; and also that nation, whom they shall 14
serve, will I judge : and afterward shall they come out
with great substance. But thou shalt go to thy fathers in 15
peace ; thou shalt be buried in a good old age. And in the 16
fourth generation they shall come hither again : for the
iniquity of the Amorite is not yet full. And it came to 17
pass, that, when the sun went down, and it was dark, behold a smoking furnace, and a flaming torch that passed
between these pieces. In that day the LORD made a 18
covenant with Abram, saying, Unto thy seed have I given
this land, from the river of Egypt unto the great river, the

---

10. the birds divided he not. Possibly as being too small, but
the reason of this part of the ritual is not known.

11. the birds of prey. Representing perhaps the forces of evil
which would make the Covenant of none effect.

12. a deep sleep: the same word as that used in ii. 21. Cf.
Job xxxiii. 15.

an horror of great darkness. The coming of God's message is
preceded by a feeling of terror. Cf. the experience of Eliphaz in
Job iv. 12–16.

13. they shall afflict them : a foretelling of the Egyptian
bondage.

16. the iniquity of the Amorite. ' The Amorite ' denotes the
original inhabitants of Palestine : see note on x. 16. The idea
expressed here is that the people must be left to work out the full
measure of their wickedness, before their punishment is inflicted.

18. the river of Egypt. Usually understood to mean the Nile,
as the word for ' river ' is generally used only of big rivers. The

19 river Euphrates: the Kenite, and the Kenizzite, and the
20 Kadmonite, and the Hittite, and the Perizzite, and the
21 Rephaim, and the Amorite, and the Canaanite, and the
Girgashite, and the Jebusite.

xvi. *The birth of Ishmael from Hagar the handmaid of Sarai.*

16   Now Sarai Abram's wife bare him no children: and she
had an handmaid, an Egyptian, whose name was Hagar.
2 And Sarai said unto Abram, Behold now, the LORD hath
restrained me from bearing; go in, I pray thee, unto my
handmaid; it may be that I shall obtain children by her.
3 And Abram hearkened to the voice of Sarai. And Sarai
Abram's wife took Hagar the Egyptian, her handmaid,
after Abram had dwelt ten years in the land of Canaan,
4 and gave her to Abram her husband to be his wife. And
he went in unto Hagar, and she conceived: and when she
saw that she had conceived, her mistress was despised in
5 her eyes. And Sarai said unto Abram, My wrong be upon
thee: I gave my handmaid into thy bosom; and when
she saw that she had conceived, I was despised in her
6 eyes: the LORD judge between me and thee. But Abram

'brook of Egypt' (Numb. xxxiv. 5 etc.) is the Wady el Arish
which ends about 45 miles S.W. of Gaza, and possibly this may
be intended here. It forms the more natural boundary of Palestine.

xvi. 1. an handmaid, a personal servant such as Bilhah was
to Rachel (xxx. 3) and Zilpah to Leah (xxx. 9). No doubt Sarai
had obtained Hagar during her sojourn in Egypt (xii. 10-20).

2. obtain children: lit. be built up, the family being regarded
as with us as a house. In Hebrew the sound of the verb suggests
the word 'children.' Sarai's expedient to obtain children was re-
sorted to also by Rachel, xxx. 3, and Leah, xxx. 9.

4. her mistress was despised. The childless woman was often
regarded with contempt, cf. 1 Sam. i. 6.

5. the LORD judge. Sarai rather unreasonably blames Abram
for Hagar's conduct. For the phrase cf. xxxi. 53; 1 Sam.
xxiv. 12.

said unto Sarai, Behold, thy maid is in thy hand; do to
her that which is good in thine eyes. And Sarai dealt
hardly with her, and she fled from her face. And the angel 7
of the LORD found her by a fountain of water in the wilderness, by the fountain in the way to Shur. And he said, Ha- 8
gar, Sarai's handmaid, whence camest thou? and whither
goest thou? And she said, I flee from the face of my mistress Sarai. And the angel of the LORD said unto her, 9
Return to thy mistress, and submit thyself under her hands.
And the angel of the LORD said unto her, I will greatly 10
multiply thy seed, that it shall not be numbered for multitude. And the angel of the LORD said unto her, Behold, 11
thou art with child, and shalt bear a son; and thou shalt
call his name Ishmael, because the LORD hath heard thy
affliction. And he shall be *as* a wild-ass among men; his 12
hand *shall be* against every man, and every man's hand
against him; and he shall dwell in the presence of all his
brethren. And she called the name of the LORD that spake 13
unto her, Thou art a God that seeth: for she said, Have

---

7. the angel of the LORD: apparently God in His revelation
form, for the promise in *v*. 10 is God's promise. In the primitive
narratives God is represented as appearing in person: it was a
feeling of reverence that later introduced the angel of the LORD
instead of Him.

the way to Shur. Shur means 'wall' but the locality is not
known. It is mentioned several times, xx. 1, xxv. 18; Exod.
xv. 22 etc.

11. Ishmael: may mean 'God hears' or 'will hear,' or possibly
'may God hear,' cf. xxi. 17. Ishmael and Isaac (cf. xvii. 19) are
the only instances in the O.T. of a name given before birth. In
the N.T. we have St John Baptist and, of course, Jesus.

12. as a wild-ass among men: lit. 'a wild-ass of a man.' The
wild-ass was quite untameable (Job xxxix. 5 ff.), and it forms a
fitting emblem of the proud unconquered Bedouin tribes which
represented the descendants of Ishmael.

in the presence: probably **over against**, i.e. in a state of con-
tinual hostility.

13. Hagar's words are quite obscure. 'A God that seeth' is
literally 'a God of seeing,' and this is intelligible. Hagar recog-

14 I even here looked after him that seeth me? Wherefore
the well was called Beer-lahai-roi; behold, it is between
15 Kadesh and Bered. And Hagar bare Abram a son: and
Abram called the name of his son, which Hagar bare,
16 Ishmael. And Abram was fourscore and six years old,
when Hagar bare Ishmael to Abram.

xvii. *The institution of Circumcision and the promises
to Abraham and Sarah.*

17 And when Abram was ninety years old and nine, the
LORD appeared to Abram, and said unto him, I am God
2 Almighty; walk before me, and be thou perfect. And I
will make my covenant between me and thee, and will

---

nized that even in the wilderness she was in God's sight. But the
next words hardly make sense. It has been proposed to emend
to 'Have I even here seen God, and lived after I have seen Him?'
More simply we might read 'Have I even here seen the seeing
God?' or even 'Has even here the seeing God seen me?'

14. Beer-lahai-roi: literally 'Well belonging to (or, 'dedicated
to') the living one who sees me.' Evidently a well with this
somewhat complicated name existed, and was supposed to per-
petuate the tradition of a Divine appearance.

xvii. It appears probable that circumcision was no new rite
even at this early stage of history, but was already practised by the
Egyptians and other nations. It is found indeed in many parts
of the world, but usually it was performed at the entrance to
manhood. With the Hebrews it signified the entrance of the
child at the earliest possible age into a covenant relation with
God. The style and language of the chapter are characteristic
of P.

1. the LORD: only here and in xxi. 1 does P use the sacred
name before Exod. vi. 2. Both instances are probably scribal
errors.

God Almighty: Hebr. El Shaddai. This is the first appearance
of a title which became fairly common, cf. xxviii. 3, xxxv. 11,
xliii. 14 etc. In the book of Job it is used very frequently, but
without the first word El. In Exod. vi. 3 it is represented as
the name by which God appeared to the patriarchs as distinguished from 'Jehovah' (Yahweh), which was first revealed to
Moses.

multiply thee exceedingly. And Abram fell on his face: 3
and God talked with him, saying, As for me, behold, my 4
covenant is with thee, and thou shalt be the father of a
multitude of nations. Neither shall thy name any more be 5
called Abram, but thy name shall be Abraham; for the
father of a multitude of nations have I made thee. And 6
I will make thee exceeding fruitful, and I will make nations of thee, and kings shall come out of thee. And I 7
will establish my covenant between me and thee and thy
seed after thee throughout their generations for an everlasting covenant, to be a God unto thee and to thy seed
after thee. And I will give unto thee, and to thy seed after 8
thee, the land of thy sojournings, all the land of Canaan,
for an everlasting possession; and I will be their God.
And God said unto Abraham, And as for thee, thou shalt 9
keep my covenant, thou, and thy seed after thee throughout their generations. This is my covenant, which ye shall 10
keep, between me and you and thy seed after thee; every
male among you shall be circumcised. And ye shall be 11
circumcised in the flesh of your foreskin; and it shall be
a token of a covenant betwixt me and you. And he that 12
is eight days old shall be circumcised among you, every
male throughout your generations, he that is born in the
house, or bought with money of any stranger, which is not
of thy seed. He that is born in thy house, and he that is 13
bought with thy money, must needs be circumcised: and
my covenant shall be in your flesh for an everlasting covenant. And the uncircumcised male who is not circumcised 14

---

5. Abraham. The change of name is the outward token of the
promise, cf. xxxii. 28 (Israel); Matt. xvi. 18 (Peter): the deriva-
tion of Abraham is uncertain, that given here resting on nothing
more than a slight similarity of sound.

6. kings shall come out of thee: a prediction of the Hebrew
monarchy.

in the flesh of his foreskin, that soul shall be cut off from his people; he hath broken my covenant.

15 And God said unto Abraham, As for Sarai thy wife, thou shalt not call her name Sarai, but Sarah shall her name be.
16 And I will bless her, and moreover I will give thee a son of her: yea, I will bless her, and she shall be *a mother of*
17 nations; kings of peoples shall be of her. Then Abraham fell upon his face, and laughed, and said in his heart, Shall a child be born unto him that is an hundred years
18 old? and shall Sarah, that is ninety years old, bear? And Abraham said unto God, Oh that Ishmael might live
19 before thee! And God said, Nay, but Sarah thy wife shall bear thee a son; and thou shalt call his name Isaac: and I will establish my covenant with him for an everlasting
20 covenant for his seed after him. And as for Ishmael, I have heard thee: behold, I have blessed him, and will make him fruitful, and will multiply him exceedingly; twelve princes shall he beget, and I will make him a great
21 nation. But my covenant will I establish with Isaac, which Sarah shall bear unto thee at this set time in the next
22 year. And he left off talking with him, and God went up
23 from Abraham. And Abraham took Ishmael his son, and all that were born in his house, and all that were bought with his money, every male among the men of Abraham's house, and circumcised the flesh of their foreskin in the

---

14. be cut off from his people. A penalty often mentioned in P. It is not certain whether it refers to death or banishment: probably the former.

15. Sarah: means 'princess,' and Sarai is probably only a more primitive form of the same word.

17. laughed. So Sarah laughed (xviii. 12) in lack of faith. But possibly in each case there is an allusion beforehand to the child's name Isaac, which means 'he laughs.'

20. twelve princes shall be beget. Their names are given in xxv. 13-15.

22. God went up. So He is represented as appearing in bodily form.

selfsame day, as God had said unto him. And Abraham 24
was ninety years old and nine, when he was circumcised
in the flesh of his foreskin. And Ishmael his son was 25
thirteen years old, when he was circumcised in the flesh
of his foreskin. In the selfsame day was Abraham cir- 26
cumcised, and Ishmael his son. And all the men of his 27
house, those born in the house, and those bought with
money of the stranger, were circumcised with him.

xviii. 1–15. *Three angels pay a visit to Abraham.*

And the LORD appeared unto him by the oaks of Mamre, **18**
as he sat in the tent door in the heat of the day; and he 2
lift up his eyes and looked, and, lo, three men stood over
against him : and when he saw them, he ran to meet them
from the tent door, and bowed himself to the earth, and 3
said, My lord, if now I have found favour in thy sight,

---

25. thirteen years old. Perhaps an indication that among the
Ishmaelite tribes circumcision was usually performed about this
age, as it is among certain Arabian tribes to-day, the Moslems
having universally adopted this rite. In modern Turkey the age
is about 9 or 10. The age among the ancient Egyptians is said
to have been 14 years.

xviii. 1–15. A passage from the earlier source, in some respects
parallel to xvii. 15–27.

1. the oaks of Mamre: i.e. at Hebron, cf. xiii. 18.

2. three men. It is difficult to explain the number. Some
have thought that it is a relic of an old tradition in which 'gods
many' figure, and have compared Ovid's story of the visit of
three gods to Hyrieus resulting in the birth of Orion. But more
probably God is conceived of as accompanied by two attendant
angels.

3. My lord. According to this rendering Abraham addresses
the central figure and does not recognize him as God. The word
however may be plural ' My lords.' The Hebrew scholars known
as the Massoretes, who added vowels to the unpointed Hebrew
text, expressly say that the word is to be read as ' My LORD,'
implying that Abraham recognized his visitor as God. This
however does not fit in with the rest of the story. Abraham's
words and actions are such as a courteous Eastern gentleman
would use towards a guest to whom he desired to shew honour.

4 pass not away, I pray thee, from thy servant: let now a
little water be fetched, and wash your feet, and rest your-
5 selves under the tree : and I will fetch a morsel of bread,
and comfort ye your heart; after that ye shall pass on :
forasmuch as ye are come to your servant. And they said,
6 So do, as thou hast said. And Abraham hastened into
the tent unto Sarah, and said, Make ready quickly three
7 measures of fine meal, knead it, and make cakes. And
Abraham ran unto the herd, and fetched a calf tender and
good, and gave it unto the servant ; and he hasted to dress
8 it. And he took butter, and milk, and the calf which he
had dressed, and set it before them ; and he stood by them
9 under the tree, and they did eat. And they said unto him,
Where is Sarah thy wife? And he said, Behold, in the
10 tent. And he said, I will certainly return unto thee when
the season cometh round ; and, lo, Sarah thy wife shall
have a son. And Sarah heard in the tent door, which was
11 behind him. Now Abraham and Sarah were old, *and*
well stricken in age ; it had ceased to be with Sarah after

---

4. wash your feet: the first duty of hospitality in the East,
xix. 2, xxiv. 32, xliii. 24 ; 1 Sam. xxv. 41; John xiii. 5.

5. comfort : used in the Old English sense of 'strengthen.' The
same Hebrew word is used of bread in Ps. civ. 15.

6. three measures: about 4 pecks, the amount used for an
ordinary baking. Cf. Matt. xiii. 33.

7. fetched a calf: a mark of special honour, for meat is not
usually eaten, cf. Luke xv. 23.

8. butter, rather **curdled milk** : a drink found refreshing in
the East, cf. Judg. v. 25.

stood by them: courteously waiting upon them.

they did eat. Only here is God said to have eaten.

10. he said. The change to the singular marks that the central
figure now takes command.

when the season cometh round : cf. *v.* 14, 2 Kings iv. 16 ff.
Usually explained as either 'this time next year' or 'when spring
comes round.' But it has been suggested that it may mean 'according to the time of child-bearing.'

11. well stricken: i.e. 'far advanced,' from an Anglo-Saxon
word. Cf. xxiv. 1; Josh. xiii. 1 ; 1 Kings i. 1.

the manner of women. And Sarah laughed within herself, 12
saying, After I am waxed old shall I have pleasure, my
lord being old also? And the LORD said unto Abraham, 13
Wherefore did Sarah laugh, saying, Shall I of a surety
bear a child, which am old? Is any thing too hard for the 14
LORD? At the set time I will return unto thee, when the
season cometh round, and Sarah shall have a son. Then 15
Sarah denied, saying, I laughed not; for she was afraid.
And he said, Nay; but thou didst laugh.

16–33. *The destruction of Sodom and Gomorrah foretold.*

And the men rose up from thence, and looked toward 16
Sodom : and Abraham went with them to bring them on
the way. And the LORD said, Shall I hide from Abraham 17
that which I do ; seeing that Abraham shall surely become 18
a great and mighty nation, and all the nations of the earth
shall be blessed in him? For I have known him, to the 19
end that he may command his children and his household after him, that they may keep the way of the LORD,
to do justice and judgement; to the end that the LORD
may bring upon Abraham that which he hath spoken of
him. And the LORD said, Because the cry of Sodom and 20
Gomorrah is great, and because their sin is very grievous;
I will go down now, and see whether they have done alto- 21
gether according to the cry of it, which is come unto me;
and if not, I will know. And the men turned from thence, 22

---

12. Sarah laughed. The repeated mention of her laughter
leads up to the name Isaac. See note on xvii. 17.

14. Is any thing too hard for the LORD? cf. Luke i. 37.

19. I have known him: i.e. taken special notice of him.
Cf. Amos iii. 2.

20. the cry of Sodom and Gomorrah. Perhaps the cities are
represented as crying for vengeance against their inhabitants,
cf. iv. 10.

and went toward Sodom: but Abraham stood yet before
23 the LORD. And Abraham drew near, and said, Wilt thou
24 consume the righteous with the wicked? Peradventure
there be fifty righteous within the city: wilt thou consume
and not spare the place for the fifty righteous that are
25 therein? That be far from thee to do after this manner,
to slay the righteous with the wicked, that so the righteous
should be as the wicked; that be far from thee: shall not
26 the Judge of all the earth do right? And the LORD said,
If I find in Sodom fifty righteous within the city, then I
27 will spare all the place for their sake. And Abraham
answered and said, Behold now, I have taken upon me to
28 speak unto the Lord, which am but dust and ashes: peradventure there shall lack five of the fifty righteous: wilt
thou destroy all the city for lack of five? And he said, I
29 will not destroy it, if I find there forty and five. And he
spake unto him yet again, and said, Peradventure there
shall be forty found there. And he said, I will not do it
30 for the forty's sake. And he said, Oh let not the Lord be
angry, and I will speak: peradventure there shall thirty
be found there. And he said, I will not do it, if I find

---

22. Abraham stood yet before the LORD. According to an
ancient tradition the original text had 'the LORD stood yet before
Abraham' (which indeed suits the context better), but this was
emended by the Scribes through motives of reverence, to 'stand
before' having acquired the association of 'serving' as in
1 Kings xvii. 1 etc.

25. the Judge of all the earth. The title Judge is applied to
God not infrequently in the Psalms, but the addition of 'all the
earth' is remarkable here. Abraham is appealing to the moral
justice of God not to involve the innocent in the punishment of
the guilty. It is an age-long problem. In this case the appearance of injustice is avoided by the rescue of Lot and his family.

28. wilt thou destroy all the city for lack of five? The
language is perhaps tinged with the recollection of Oriental bar-
gaining, but in its earnestness and simplicity it would be hard to
find a better instance of intercessory prayer. Cf. also Exod. xxxii.
11-14, 31, 32.

thirty there. And he said, Behold now, I have taken upon 31
me to speak unto the Lord: peradventure there shall be
twenty found there. And he said, I will not destroy it for
the twenty's sake. And he said, Oh let not the Lord be 32
angry, and I will speak yet but this once: peradventure
ten shall be found there. And he said, I will not destroy
it for the ten's sake. And the LORD went his way, as soon 33
as he had left communing with Abraham: and Abraham
returned unto his place.

xix. *The destruction of the Cities of the Plain,*
and the rescue of Lot.

And the two angels came to Sodom at even; and Lot **19**
sat in the gate of Sodom: and Lot saw them, and rose up
to meet them; and he bowed himself with his face to the
earth; and he said, Behold now, my lords, turn aside, I 2
pray you, into your servant's house, and tarry all night,
and wash your feet, and ye shall rise up early, and go on
your way. And they said, Nay; but we will abide in the
street all night. And he urged them greatly; and they 3
turned in unto him, and entered into his house; and he

---

33. communing with Abraham: the verb means nothing more
than 'speaking unto' Abraham.

xix. The story with which the chapter begins serves to illustrate
the incurable wickedness of the people of Sodom, and to bring
out the justice of the overthrow of the city. Emphasis is laid on
Lot's hospitality which in the East is accounted for righteousness.
To protect his guests he is willing to sacrifice his own daughters.
To our minds this would seem a strange perversion, but it would
probably be regarded as meritorious in the East, where the
position of women is often very unsatisfactory.

1. the two angels. God had returned to heaven (xviii. 33),
leaving His angelic attendants on earth.

2. turn aside. Lot in his eager hospitality 'entertained angels
unawares,' Hebr. xiii. 2.

in the street: rather 'the open space' near the gate of a
city.

made them a feast, and did bake unleavened bread, and
4 they did eat. But before they lay down, the men of the
city, *even* the men of Sodom, compassed the house round,
both young and old, all the people from every quarter;
5 and they called unto Lot, and said unto him, Where are
the men which came in to thee this night? bring them out
6 unto us, that we may know them. And Lot went out unto
7 them to the door, and shut the door after him. And he
8 said, I pray you, my brethren, do not so wickedly. Behold
now, I have two daughters which have not known man;
let me, I pray you, bring them out unto you, and do ye to
them as is good in your eyes: only unto these men do
nothing; forasmuch as they are come under the shadow
9 of my roof. And they said, Stand back. And they said,
This one fellow came in to sojourn, and he will needs be a
judge: now will we deal worse with thee, than with them.
And they pressed sore upon the man, even Lot, and drew
10 near to break the door. But the men put forth their hand,
and brought Lot into the house to them, and shut to the
11 door. And they smote the men that were at the door of
the house with blindness, both small and great: so that
12 they wearied themselves to find the door. And the men
said unto Lot, Hast thou here any besides? son in law,
and thy sons, and thy daughters, and whomsoever thou
13 hast in the city; bring them out of the place: for we will
destroy this place, because the cry of them is waxen great
before the LORD; and the LORD hath sent us to destroy
14 it. And Lot went out, and spake unto his sons in law,
which married his daughters, and said, Up, get you out of

---

9. This one fellow. Lot is a stranger, and has not associated
with the men of the city.

10. the men: i.e. the two angels. See note on *v.* 1.

11. blindness: a special word denoting supernatural blindness,
found elsewhere only in 2 Kings vi. 18.

14. which married: R.V. marg. *which were to marry* seems
better.

this place; for the LORD will destroy the city. But he
seemed unto his sons in law as one that mocked. And 15
when the morning arose, then the angels hastened Lot,
saying, Arise, take thy wife, and thy two daughters which
are here; lest thou be consumed in the iniquity of the city.
But he lingered; and the men laid hold upon his hand, 16
and upon the hand of his wife, and upon the hand of his
two daughters; the LORD being merciful unto him: and
they brought him forth, and set him without the city. And 17
it came to pass, when they had brought them forth
abroad, that he said, Escape for thy life; look not behind thee, neither stay thou in all the Plain; escape to
the mountain, lest thou be consumed. And Lot said 18
unto them, Oh, not so, my lord: behold now, thy ser- 19
vant hath found grace in thy sight, and thou hast mag-
nified thy mercy, which thou hast shewed unto me in
saving my life; and I cannot escape to the mountain,
lest evil overtake me, and I die: behold now, this city 20
is near to flee unto, and it is a little one: Oh, let me
escape thither, (is it not a little one?) and my soul shall
live. And he said unto him, See, I have accepted thee 21
concerning this thing also, that I will not overthrow the
city of which thou hast spoken. Haste thee, escape thither; 22
for I cannot do any thing till thou be come thither. Therefore the name of the city was called Zoar. The sun was 23
risen upon the earth when Lot came unto Zoar. Then the 24

---

16. he lingered. Perhaps unwilling to abandon his earthly
wealth. Lot is a type of the 'double minded man.' (Jas. i. 8.)

17. to the mountain: i.e. the hills of Moab. There the very
atmosphere would be a contrast to the shaming cities of the
Plain. But Lot is no mountain dweller: he feels that he cannot
at present live outside a city. Later his fear drives him to the
mountain (v. 30).

20. a little one. Zoar means 'little.'

22. Zoar: in xiv. 2 identified with Bela. In Isa. xv. 5; Jer.
xlviii. 34 it is called a Moabite city. It seems to have been
situated near the S.E. corner of the Dead Sea.

LORD rained upon Sodom and upon Gomorrah brimstone
25 and fire from the LORD out of heaven ; and he overthrew
those cities, and all the Plain, and all the inhabitants of
26 the cities, and that which grew upon the ground. But his
wife looked back from behind him, and she became a
27 pillar of salt. And Abraham gat up early in the morning
28 to the place where he had stood before the LORD : and he
looked toward Sodom and Gomorrah, and toward all the
land of the Plain, and beheld, and, lo, the smoke of the
land went up as the smoke of a furnace.

29   And it came to pass, when God destroyed the cities of
the Plain, that God remembered Abraham, and sent Lot
out of the midst of the overthrow, when he overthrew the
cities in the which Lot dwelt.

30–38. *The origin of Moab and Ammon.*

30   And Lot went up out of Zoar, and dwelt in the mountain,
and his two daughters with him ; for he feared to dwell in
Zoar : and he dwelt in a cave, he and his two daughters.
31 And the firstborn said unto the younger, Our father is old,

---

24. brimstone and fire: the two are often found together,
Ps. xi. 6; Ezek. xxxviii. 22; Rev. ix. 17, xx. 10, xxi. 8. It has
been thought that the catastrophe might have been caused by an
earthquake, but there is no mention of this.

26. his wife looked back: apparently yearning after the old
life. Our Lord's use of this illustration (Luke xvii. 32) is very
impressive.

a pillar of salt. Such pillars of crystallized rock salt are not
uncommon in the neighbourhood, and some represent faithfully
the shape of human figures.

29. when God destroyed. The story of the overthrow of
Sodom and Gomorrah made a deep impression on the Jews. For
Biblical references compare among others Deut. xxix. 23 ; Isa. i. 9
(quoted in Rom. ix. 29), xiii. 19; Jer. xlix. 48; Amos iv. 11;
Matt. x. 15 etc. ; 2 Pet. ii. 6=Jude 7.

30–38. This unpleasant story need not be taken as literal history.
It seems designed to shew that Moab and Ammon were kindred
nations to the Israelites, but markedly inferior to them.

and there is not a man in the earth to come in unto us
after the manner of all the earth: come, let us make our 32
father drink wine, and we will lie with him, that we may
preserve seed of our father. And they made their father 33
drink wine that night: and the firstborn went in, and lay
with her father; and he knew not when she lay down,
nor when she arose. And it came to pass on the morrow, 34
that the firstborn said unto the younger, Behold, I lay
yesternight with my father: let us make him drink wine
this night also; and go thou in, and lie with him, that we
may preserve seed of our father. And they made their 35
father drink wine that night also: and the younger arose,
and lay with him; and he knew not when she lay down,
nor when she arose. Thus were both the daughters of 36
Lot with child by their father. And the firstborn bare a 37
son, and called his name Moab: the same is the father
of the Moabites unto this day. And the younger, she also 38
bare a son, and called his name Ben-ammi: the same is
the father of the children of Ammon unto this day.

xx. *Abraham and Sarah at Gerar.*

And Abraham journeyed from thence toward the land **20**
of the South, and dwelt between Kadesh and Shur; and
he sojourned in Gerar. And Abraham said of Sarah his 2
wife, She is my sister: and Abimelech king of Gerar sent,

---

xx. It will be noticed that there are two other stories of a similar
character to this, one (xii. 10-20) related of Abraham, the other
(xxvi. 6-11) of Isaac. The latter is said to have happened also at
Gerar, and the resemblance is close. It seems natural to suppose
that we have here an instance of a tradition repeated in similar
form once if not twice. The story is interesting as revealing a
very high moral standard in a small heathen kingdom. Indeed
the character of Abimelech in this section compares very favour-
ably with that of Abraham.

2. Abimelech. The name means 'Melech is my father.' The
same root occurs in Molech and Milcom. The similar name
Abi-milki occurs in the Tel-el-Amarna tablets as the name of
an Egyptian Governor of Tyre (c. 1400 B.C.).

3 and took Sarah. But God came to Abimelech in a dream
of the night, and said to him, Behold, thou art but a dead
man, because of the woman which thou hast taken; for
4 she is a man's wife. Now Abimelech had not come near
her : and he said, Lord, wilt thou slay even a righteous
5 nation? Said he not himself unto me, She is my sister?
and she, even she herself said, He is my brother : in the
integrity of my heart and the innocency of my hands have
6 I done this. And God said unto him in the dream, Yea,
I know that in the integrity of thy heart thou hast done
this, and I also withheld thee from sinning against me :
7 therefore suffered I thee not to touch her. Now therefore
restore the man's wife; for he is a prophet, and he shall
pray for thee, and thou shalt live : and if thou restore her
not, know thou that thou shalt surely die, thou, and all
8 that are thine. And Abimelech rose early in the morning,
and called all his servants, and told all these things in
9 their ears : and the men were sore afraid. Then Abimelech called Abraham, and said unto him, What hast thou
done unto us? and wherein have I sinned against thee,
that thou hast brought on me and on my kingdom a great
sin? thou hast done deeds unto me that ought not to be
10 done. And Abimelech said unto Abraham, What sawest
11 thou, that thou hast done this thing? And Abraham said,

---

took Sarah : i.e. into his harem.

3. in a dream. The passage comes from the source called E,
and it is characteristic that God's message is conveyed in a
dream.

7. he is a prophet. This is the first occurrence of the word
'prophet,' and it does not seem to be used quite in the ordinary
sense of the bearer of God's message, but rather of a holy man
whose intercession would be effective. In Ps. cv. 15 (which
apparently refers to this passage) the patriarchs generally are
called prophets.

9. a great sin. The taking of a married woman into the king's
harem, although done unwittingly, is regarded as a great sin that
might have brought retribution on the whole kingdom.

Because I thought, Surely the fear of God is not in this place; and they will slay me for my wife's sake. And 12 moreover she is indeed my sister, the daughter of my father, but not the daughter of my mother; and she became my wife: and it came to pass, when God caused me 13 to wander from my father's house, that I said unto her, This is thy kindness which thou shalt shew unto me; at every place whither we shall come, say of me, He is my brother. And Abimelech took sheep and oxen, and men- 14 servants and womenservants, and gave them unto Abraham, and restored him Sarah his wife. And Abimelech said, 15 Behold, my land is before thee: dwell where it pleaseth thee. And unto Sarah he said, Behold, I have given thy 16 brother a thousand pieces of silver: behold, it is for thee a covering of the eyes to all that are with thee; and in respect of all thou art righted. And Abraham prayed unto 17 God: and God healed Abimelech, and his wife, and his maidservants; and they bare children. For the LORD had 18 fast closed up all the wombs of the house of Abimelech, because of Sarah Abraham's wife.

xxi. 1–7. *The birth of Isaac.*

And the LORD visited Sarah as he had said, and the **21** LORD did unto Sarah as he had spoken. And Sarah con- 2 ceived, and bare Abraham a son in his old age, at the set

---

11. the fear of God. The more common expression is 'the fear of the LORD,' which occurs 13 times in Proverbs, and in Prov. i. 7 = Ps. cxi. 10 (cf. Job xxviii. 28) is represented as the beginning of wisdom. A place without 'the fear of God' is an uncivilized and heathen place.

12. she became my wife. Marriage with a half-sister was apparently not uncommon among the peoples of Canaan.

16. a covering of the eyes. Sarah's relatives might consider themselves bound to avenge the wrong done to her, so the liberal present is designed to 'shut their eyes' to the wrong.

17. Abraham prayed. A second instance of successful intercession in the story of Abraham.

xxi. 1. the LORD visited Sarah. God's visitations are some-

3 time of which God had spoken to him. And Abraham
　called the name of his son that was born unto him, whom
4 Sarah bare to him, Isaac. And Abraham circumcised his
　son Isaac when he was eight days old, as God had com-
5 manded him. And Abraham was an hundred years old,
6 when his son Isaac was born unto him. And Sarah said,
　God hath made me to laugh; every one that heareth will
7 laugh with me. And she said, Who would have said unto
　Abraham, that Sarah should give children suck? for I
　have borne him a son in his old age.

8-21. *The expulsion of Hagar and Ishmael.*

8　　And the child grew, and was weaned: and Abraham
　made a great feast on the day that Isaac was weaned.
9 And Sarah saw the son of Hagar the Egyptian, which she
10 had borne unto Abraham, mocking. Wherefore she said
　unto Abraham, Cast out this bondwoman and her son:

---

times for blessing as here (cf. 1 Sam. ii. 21; Luke i. 68), and
sometimes for punishment. Cf. Exod. xx. 5; Job xxxv. 15;
Ps. lxxxix. 32.

6. God hath made me to laugh. The use of 'God' instead
of 'the LORD' indicates that this verse comes from E. The
connection of the name Isaac with laughter has already been
traced in P (xvii. 17) and J (xviii. 12).

8-21. The story is one of the most vivid and picturesque in
Genesis, and reveals the hand of the writer of the more ancient
source (J).

8. a great feast. Such was common on the occasion of the
weaning of a child, which might be as late as his third or fourth
year.

9. mocking. The marg. 'playing' is to be preferred, though
Jewish writers imagine that Ishmael was illtreating Isaac in
various ways. Hence St Paul's idea in Gal. iv. 29. According
to the account before us Ishmael was only a little lad who could
ride on his mother's shoulder (*v.* 15). But of course he would be
bigger and stronger than Isaac, and this seems to have aroused
Sarah's jealousy. She may also have resented the idea that the
boys should grow up together.

10. Cast out this bondwoman. St Paul's allegorical use of
this verse in Gal. iv. 30 is very typical of his use of the O.T.

for the son of this bondwoman shall not be heir with my
son, even with Isaac. And the thing was very grievous in 11
Abraham's sight on account of his son. And God said 12
unto Abraham, Let it not be grievous in thy sight because
of the lad, and because of thy bondwoman; in all that
Sarah saith unto thee, hearken unto her voice; for in Isaac
shall thy seed be called. And also of the son of the bond- 13
woman will I make a nation, because he is thy seed. And 14
Abraham rose up early in the morning, and took bread
and a bottle of water, and gave it unto Hagar, putting it
on her shoulder, and the child, and sent her away: and
she departed, and wandered in the wilderness of Beer-
sheba. And the water in the bottle was spent, and she 15
cast the child under one of the shrubs. And she went, 16
and sat her down over against him a good way off, as it
were a bowshot: for she said, Let me not look upon the
death of the child. And she sat over against him, and lift
up her voice, and wept. And God heard the voice of the 17
lad; and the angel of God called to Hagar out of heaven,
and said unto her, What aileth thee, Hagar? fear not; for
God hath heard the voice of the lad where he is. Arise, 18
lift up the lad, and hold him in thine hand; for I will
make him a great nation. And God opened her eyes, and 19
she saw a well of water; and she went, and filled the

---

11. on account of his son. A very human touch, implying
Abraham's pride in the elder boy.

13. will I make a nation. A renewal of the promise made to
Hagar in xvi. 10. Cf. xxi. 18.

14. a bottle of water: rather 'a skin' such as are still used
in Cairo and other Eastern cities. They hold a large quantity of
water, and are correspondingly heavy.

Beer-sheba: nearly 30 miles S.W. of Hebron. In the Great
War its water supply was of great value first for the Turks and
then for the British. It is frequently mentioned as the southern-
most town in the land in the phrase 'from Dan even unto Beer-
sheba.' 1 Sam. iii. 20 etc.

17. God heard. An allusion to the meaning of Ishmael. Cf.
xvi. 11.

20 bottle with water, and gave the lad drink. And God was
with the lad, and he grew; and he dwelt in the wilderness,
21 and became an archer. And he dwelt in the wilderness of
Paran: and his mother took him a wife out of the land of
Egypt.

22–34. *Abraham's treaty with Abimelech at Beer-sheba.*

22 And it came to pass at that time, that Abimelech and
Phicol the captain of his host spake unto Abraham, saying,
23 God is with thee in all that thou doest: now therefore
swear unto me here by God that thou wilt not deal falsely
with me, nor with my son, nor with my son's son: but
according to the kindness that I have done unto thee,
thou shalt do unto me, and to the land wherein thou hast
$^{24}_{25}$ sojourned. And Abraham said, I will swear. And Abraham reproved Abimelech because of the well of water,
which Abimelech's servants had violently taken away.
26 And Abimelech said, I know not who hath done this thing:
neither didst thou tell me, neither yet heard I of it, but
27 to-day. And Abraham took sheep and oxen, and gave
them unto Abimelech; and they two made a covenant.
28 And Abraham set seven ewe lambs of the flock by them-

---

21. the wilderness of Paran: the wild and desolate country
at the extreme S. of the land.

his mother took him a wife. It was the parents' business to
find a wife for their son. Cf. xxiv. 3, xxxiv. 4; Judg. xiv. 2.

out of the land of Egypt: she naturally chose a woman of her
own country. Cf. xvi. 1.

22–34. The passage is a further indication of Abraham's power
and importance.

23. nor with my son, nor with my son's son. R.V. marg.
'my offspring, nor with my posterity' indicates that the words
used are not the usual ones. They occur together again in Job
xviii. 19; Isa. xiv. 22. In this passage they seem to have a legal
ring which is in accordance with the terms of a treaty.

28. seven ewe lambs. Two derivations of Beer-sheba seem
conjoined in this passage, 'well of seven' or 'well of swearing'
(*v.* 31, cf. also xxvi. 31–33). The first seems more likely to be

selves. And Abimelech said unto Abraham, What mean 29
these seven ewe lambs which thou hast set by themselves?
And he said, These seven ewe lambs shalt thou take of 30
my hand, that it may be a witness unto me, that I have
digged this well. Wherefore he called that place Beer- 31
sheba; because there they sware both of them. So they 32
made a covenant at Beer-sheba: and Abimelech rose up,
and Phicol the captain of his host, and they returned into
the land of the Philistines. And *Abraham* planted a tama- 33
risk tree in Beer-sheba, and called there on the name of
the LORD, the Everlasting God. And Abraham sojourned 34
in the land of the Philistines many days.

> xxii. 1-19. *Abraham prepares to offer up Isaac*
> *in obedience to a Divine command.*

And it came to pass after these things, that God did **22**
prove Abraham, and said unto him, Abraham; and he
said, Here am I. And he said, Take now thy son, thine 2
only son, whom thou lovest, even Isaac, and get thee into
the land of Moriah; and offer him there for a burnt offer-

---

original, as there are seven wells here at the present time. But
the word 'seven' apparently lies behind the Hebrew word 'to
swear an oath' which means literally 'to bind one's self by seven
things.'

32. into the land of the Philistines. Strictly an anachronism,
for the Philistines did not migrate into Palestine from Caphtor
till many years later. See note on x. 14.

xxii. 1-19. The sacrifice of children was not unknown among
surrounding nations at this and later times (cf. 2 Kings iii. 27,
xvii. 31), and even among the Israelites (Micah vi. 7). Hence
it would not seem to Abraham so incredible that God should de-
mand the sacrifice of Isaac as it does to us.

1. prove: i.e. put to the test. Cf. Exod. xvi. 4; Deut.
viii. 16.

2. the land of Moriah. The locality is unknown. In 2 Chr.
iii. 1 mount Moriah stands for Jerusalem, but the name Moriah
is probably designed from this passage, and has little geographical
value. Jerusalem was not a bare hill, but a town, as early as
Abraham's time. One version has 'the land of the Amorites.'

ing upon one of the mountains which I will tell thee of.
3 And Abraham rose early in the morning, and saddled his
ass, and took two of his young men with him, and Isaac
his son; and he clave the wood for the burnt offering, and
rose up, and went unto the place of which God had told
4 him. On the third day Abraham lifted up his eyes, and
5 saw the place afar off. And Abraham said unto his young
men, Abide ye here with the ass, and I and the lad will
go yonder; and we will worship, and come again to you.
6 And Abraham took the wood of the burnt offering, and
laid it upon Isaac his son; and he took in his hand the
fire and the knife; and they went both of them together.
7 And Isaac spake unto Abraham his father, and said,
My father: and he said, Here am I, my son. And he
said, Behold, the fire and the wood: but where is the
8 lamb for a burnt offering? And Abraham said, God will
provide himself the lamb for a burnt offering, my son:
9 so they went both of them together. And they came
to the place which God had told him of; and Abraham
built the altar there, and laid the wood in order, and
bound Isaac his son, and laid him on the altar, upon
10 the wood. And Abraham stretched forth his hand, and
11 took the knife to slay his son. And the angel of the LORD
called unto him out of heaven, and said, Abraham, Abra-
12 ham: and he said, Here am I. And he said, Lay not thine
hand upon the lad, neither do thou any thing unto him:

---

3. clave the wood: apparently he expected as his destination
a desolate mountain without trees. There was however a thicket
there (*v.* 13).

8. God will provide himself: lit. see (or look out) for himself.
The verb seems to anticipate Jehovah-jireh (*v.* 14).

9. bound Isaac: the verb is not found elsewhere in the O.T.,
but in later Hebrew it is often used of binding an animal for
sacrifice. Isaac in his willing obedience is a true type of Christ,
who offered Himself for us. Tertullian sees in *v.* 6 a type of Christ
bearing His cross, while Augustine regards the ram that was
offered instead of Isaac as pointing forward to the Death of Christ.

for now I know that thou fearest God, seeing thou hast
not withheld thy son, thine only son, from me. And Ab- 13
raham lifted up his eyes, and looked, and behold, behind
him a ram caught in the thicket by his horns: and Abraham went and took the ram, and offered him up for a
burnt offering in the stead of his son. And Abraham called 14
the name of that place Jehovah-jireh : as it is said to this
day, In the mount of the LORD it shall be provided. And 15
the angel of the LORD called unto Abraham a second
time out of heaven, and said, By myself have I sworn, 16
saith the LORD, because thou hast done this thing, and
hast not withheld thy son, thine only son : that in blessing 17
I will bless thee, and in multiplying I will multiply thy
seed as the stars of the heaven, and as the sand which is
upon the sea shore ; and thy seed shall possess the gate
of his enemies; and in thy seed shall all the nations of 18
the earth be blessed ; because thou hast obeyed my voice.
So Abraham returned unto his young men, and they rose 19
up and went together to Beer-sheba ; and Abraham dwelt
at Beer-sheba.

20-24. *The children of Nahor.*

And it came to pass after these things, that it was told 20
Abraham, saying, Behold, Milcah, she also hath borne
children unto thy brother Nahor; Uz his firstborn, and 21

---

14. it shall be provided. The meaning is not certainly known.
We have at any rate two alternatives : (1) in the mount of the
LORD He is seen, or (2) in the mount of the LORD it is provided.
The latter agrees best with the meaning of Jehovah-jireh 'the
LORD sees or provides.' The mount would naturally be called
'the mount of the LORD' from this story, and the fact that this
expression is applied to Jerusalem, or rather the Temple hill in
Ps. xxiv. 3 ; Isa. ii. 3 etc., would be sufficient to account for the
story that the (unfulfilled) sacrifice of Isaac took place on the
spot where the Temple was built later.

18. in thy seed…blessed. Cf. xii. 3, xviii. 18.

20-24. The list of names contains several that are otherwise
unknown. Milcah in xi. 27, 29 appears as the niece of Nahor.

22 Buz his brother, and Kemuel the father of Aram; and Chesed, and Hazo, and Pildash, and Jidlaph, and Bethuel.
23 And Bethuel begat Rebekah: these eight did Milcah bear
24 to Nahor, Abraham's brother. And his concubine, whose name was Reumah, she also bare Tebah, and Gaham, and Tahash, and Maacah.

xxiii. *The death and burial of Sarah.*

23 And the life of Sarah was an hundred and seven and twenty years: these were the years of the life of Sarah.
2 And Sarah died in Kiriath-arba (the same is Hebron), in the land of Canaan: and Abraham came to mourn for
3 Sarah, and to weep for her. And Abraham rose up from before his dead, and spake unto the children of Heth,
4 saying, I am a stranger and a sojourner with you: give me a possession of a buryingplace with you, that I may
5 bury my dead out of my sight. And the children of Heth
6 answered Abraham, saying unto him, Hear us, my lord: thou art a mighty prince among us: in the choice of our sepulchres bury thy dead; none of us shall withhold from

---

Uz is mentioned again in x. 23. Buz comes before us in the book of Job as the birthplace of Elihu.

A list such as this has its main interest in shewing the ideas current as to the relationship of tribes and clans.

xxiii. Abraham's first possession in the Land of Promise was but a burying place. This chapter, written in the formal style of P, relates how this was acquired.

2. Kiriath-arba: lit. 'the city of four': possibly four different peoples had their quarters in it. It is P's regular name for Hebron which itself means Confederacy. It has been thought that Arba was the name of an old Canaanite god.

3. the children of Heth: i.e. the Hittites, a great nation who from their capital in the wilds of Armenia founded an empire that at one time reached as far as the Mediterranean. It would appear that a small and isolated branch may have settled at Hebron. Possibly, however, as Driver suggests, after the disappearance of the Hittites from history their name may have been applied vaguely to the ancient peoples of Palestine.

6. in the choice of our sepulchres. The whole story throws

thee his sepulchre, but that thou mayest bury thy dead.
And Abraham rose up, and bowed himself to the people 7
of the land, even to the children of Heth. And he com- 8
muned with them, saying, If it be your mind that I should
bury my dead out of my sight, hear me, and intreat for
me to Ephron the son of Zohar, that he may give me the 9
cave of Machpelah, which he hath, which is in the end of
his field; for the full price let him give it to me in the
midst of you for a possession of a buryingplace. Now 10
Ephron was sitting in the midst of the children of Heth:
and Ephron the Hittite answered Abraham in the audience
of the children of Heth, even of all that went in at the
gate of his city, saying, Nay, my lord, hear me: the field 11
give I thee, and the cave that is therein, I give it thee;
in the presence of the sons of my people give I it thee:
bury thy dead. And Abraham bowed himself down before 12
the people of the land. And he spake unto Ephron in the 13
audience of the people of the land, saying, But if thou wilt,
I pray thee, hear me: I will give the price of the field;
take it of me, and I will bury my dead there. And Ephron 14
answered Abraham, saying unto him, My lord, hearken 15
unto me: a piece of land worth four hundred shekels of
silver, what is that betwixt me and thee? bury therefore

---

an interesting sidelight on the courtesy of Oriental business. The
offer is probably not intended to be taken literally, but Abraham
acknowledges it by a low obeisance (*vv.* 7, 12). Finally after a
further interchange of courtesies a price is fixed and accepted.

9. the cave of Machpelah: the name means 'double,' signifying
perhaps that there was room for two bodies to lie there. Cf. xxv. 9.
Caves were often used for burial. So Christ was laid in a cave
tomb. Compare also the Tombs of the Kings in the rocky gorge
near Luxor.

15. four hundred shekels of silver: the value would be about
£55. It is noticeable that the money is uncoined, and has to be
weighed. No Jewish coins were minted before the 2nd cent. B.C.,
but the silver was apparently used for currency in bars stamped
with a certain weight. The Phœnicians are said to have been
the first to do this.

16 thy dead. And Abraham hearkened unto Ephron; and
Abraham weighed to Ephron the silver, which he had
named in the audience of the children of Heth, four hundred shekels of silver, current *money* with the merchant.

17 So the field of Ephron, which was in Machpelah, which
was before Mamre, the field, and the cave which was
therein, and all the trees that were in the field, that
were in all the border thereof round about, were made

18 sure unto Abraham for a possession in the presence of
the children of Heth, before all that went in at the gate

19 of his city. And after this, Abraham buried Sarah his wife
in the cave of the field of Machpelah before Mamre (the

20 same is Hebron), in the land of Canaan. And the field,
and the cave that is therein, were made sure unto Abraham for a possession of a buryingplace by the children of
Heth.

> xxiv. *Abraham's servant fetches Rebekah from
> Mesopotamia to be Isaac's wife.*

24   And Abraham was old, *and* well stricken in age : and

2 the LORD had blessed Abraham in all things. And Abraham said unto his servant, the elder of his house, that
ruled over all that he had, Put, I pray thee, thy hand under

3 my thigh : and I will make thee swear by the LORD, the

---

17. were made sure: probably by a signed contract. *Vv.* 17
and 18 are obviously couched in legal language, such as is common
in deeds of sale of all periods. The contract was duly witnessed
by the children of Heth. Cf. Ruth iv. 9–11; Jerem. xxxii. 12.
In this burial place Abraham himself was buried (xxv. 9), and
afterwards Isaac (xxxv. 27, 29), Rebekah and Leah (xlix. 31),
and Jacob (l. 23).

xxiv. The story is told with life-like simplicity, and illustrates
in many respects the marriage customs of the East.

2. the elder of his house. The steward in a rich man's house
had nearly everything under his control. It is this trust that is
a special feature in the Parable of the Unjust Steward (Luke xvi.).
In xv. 2 Abraham's steward is called Eliezer.

Put...thy hand under my thigh. This symbolical action in

God of heaven and the God of the earth, that thou shalt
not take a wife for my son of the daughters of the Canaanites, among whom I dwell: but thou shalt go unto my 4
country, and to my kindred, and take a wife for my son
Isaac. And the servant said unto him, Peradventure the 5
woman will not be willing to follow me unto this land:
must I needs bring thy son again unto the land from
whence thou camest? And Abraham said unto him, Be- 6
ware thou that thou bring not my son thither again. The 7
LORD, the God of heaven, that took me from my father's
house, and from the land of my nativity, and that spake
unto me, and that sware unto me, saying, Unto thy seed
will I give this land; he shall send his angel before thee,
and thou shalt take a wife for my son from thence. And 8
if the woman be not willing to follow thee, then thou shalt
be clear from this my oath; only thou shalt not bring my
son thither again. And the servant put his hand under 9
the thigh of Abraham his master, and sware to him concerning this matter. And the servant took ten camels, of 10
the camels of his master, and departed; having all goodly
things of his master's in his hand: and he arose, and
went to Mesopotamia, unto the city of Nahor. And he 11
made the camels to kneel down without the city by the
well of water at the time of evening, the time that women
go out to draw water. And he said, O LORD, the God of 12
my master Abraham, send me, I pray thee, good speed
this day, and shew kindness unto my master Abraham.

---

taking an oath is supposed to bind not only the one who swears
but also his descendants. It occurs again in xlvii. 29. A similar
custom is said to exist among the aborigines of Australia.

6. bring not my son thither again. For Isaac to return to
Haran would be almost to turn his back on God's promises.

7. send his angel before thee: i.e. that everything may be
prepared for the success of thy visit.

11. women go out to draw water: cf. Exod. ii. 16; 1 Sam.
ix. 11; John iv. 7. Such is still the custom in the East.

13 Behold, I stand by the fountain of water; and the daugh-
14 ters of the men of the city come out to draw water: and
let it come to pass, that the damsel to whom I shall say,
Let down thy pitcher, I pray thee, that I may drink; and
she shall say, Drink, and I will give thy camels drink also:
let the same be she that thou hast appointed for thy servant Isaac; and thereby shall I know that thou hast
15 shewed kindness unto my master. And it came to pass,
before he had done speaking, that, behold, Rebekah came
out, who was born to Bethuel the son of Milcah, the wife
of Nahor, Abraham's brother, with her pitcher upon her
16 shoulder. And the damsel was very fair to look upon, a
virgin, neither had any man known her: and she went
down to the fountain, and filled her pitcher, and came up.
17 And the servant ran to meet her, and said, Give me to
18 drink, I pray thee, a little water of thy pitcher. And she
said, Drink, my lord: and she hasted, and let down her
19 pitcher upon her hand, and gave him drink. And when
she had done giving him drink, she said, I will draw for
20 thy camels also, until they have done drinking. And she
hasted, and emptied her pitcher into the trough, and ran
again unto the well to draw, and drew for all his camels.
21 And the man looked stedfastly on her; holding his peace,
to know whether the LORD had made his journey pros-
22 perous or not. And it came to pass, as the camels had
done drinking, that the man took a golden ring of half a

---

14. The servant asks for a sign to be given that he may know
which maiden God has intended to be the wife of his master's
son. To respond at once to the request for water, and to proceed
further to water the camels for a stranger, would imply a very
kindly and considerate nature.

19. until they have done drinking. A camel can go several
days without water, but when it drinks it requires many gallons
to slake its thirst. Hence Rebekah's task was no light one, to
provide as much water as was wanted for ten camels.

22. a golden ring: lit. a golden nose ring such as women stil

shekel weight, and two bracelets for her hands of ten
shekels weight of gold ; and said, Whose daughter art 23
thou? tell me, I pray thee. Is there room in thy father's
house for us to lodge in? And she said unto him, I am 24
the daughter of Bethuel the son of Milcah, which she
bare unto Nahor. She said moreover unto him, We have 25
both straw and provender enough, and room to lodge in.
And the man bowed his head, and worshipped the LORD. 26
And he said, Blessed be the LORD, the God of my master 27
Abraham, who hath not forsaken his mercy and his truth
toward my master : as for me, the LORD hath led me in
the way to the house of my master's brethren. And the 28
damsel ran, and told her mother's house according to
these words. And Rebekah had a brother, and his name 29
was Laban : and Laban ran out unto the man, unto the
fountain. And it came to pass, when he saw the ring, and 30
the bracelets upon his sister's hands, and when he heard
the words of Rebekah his sister, saying, Thus spake the
man unto me ; that he came unto the man ; and, behold,
he stood by the camels at the fountain. And he said, Come 31
in, thou blessed of the LORD ; wherefore standest thou
without? for I have prepared the house, and room for the
camels. And the man came into the house, and he ungird- 32
ed the camels ; and he gave straw and provender for the

---

wear, cf. *v.* 47. The gifts were first of all a return for her
kindness.

26. worshipped the LORD : i.e. in thankfulness. The simple
piety of the servant comes out in all that he does.

28. her mother's house. As was common in the East,
Rebekah's mother had a separate tent and establishment.

30. when he saw the ring. Laban's first appearance reveals
his character as that of a man always on the look out to reap an
advantage. Throughout this story he takes the lead rather than
Bethuel. Cf. *vv.* 50, 55, 60.

32. he ungirded the camels. He sees to the comfort of his
beasts before his own, and when that is done he will not eat till
he has delivered his message.

camels, and water to wash his feet and the men's feet that
33 were with him. And there was set meat before him to eat:
but he said, I will not eat, until I have told mine errand.
34 And he said, Speak on. And he said, I am Abraham's
35 servant. And the LORD hath blessed my master greatly;
and he is become great: and he hath given him flocks
and herds, and silver and gold, and menservants and
36 maidservants, and camels and asses. And Sarah my
master's wife bare a son to my master when she was old:
37 and unto him hath he given all that he hath. And my
master made me swear, saying, Thou shalt not take a wife
for my son of the daughters of the Canaanites, in whose
38 land I dwell: but thou shalt go unto my father's house,
39 and to my kindred, and take a wife for my son. And I
said unto my master, Peradventure the woman will not
40 follow me. And he said unto me, The LORD, before
whom I walk, will send his angel with thee, and prosper
thy way; and thou shalt take a wife for my son of my
41 kindred, and of my father's house: then shalt thou be
clear from my oath, when thou comest to my kindred; and
if they give her not to thee, thou shalt be clear from my
42 oath. And I came this day unto the fountain, and said,
O LORD, the God of my master Abraham, if now thou do
43 prosper my way which I go: behold, I stand by the fountain of water; and let it come to pass, that the maiden
which cometh forth to draw, to whom I shall say, Give
44 me, I pray thee, a little water of thy pitcher to drink; and
she shall say to me, Both drink thou, and I will also draw
for thy camels: let the same be the woman whom the
45 LORD hath appointed for my master's son. And before I
had done speaking in mine heart, behold, Rebekah came
forth with her pitcher on her shoulder; and she went down
unto the fountain, and drew: and I said unto her, Let me
46 drink, I pray thee. And she made haste, and let down
her pitcher from her shoulder, and said, Drink, and I

will give thy camels drink also: so I drank, and she made
the camels drink also. And I asked her, and said, Whose 47
daughter art thou? And she said, The daughter of Bethuel, Nahor's son, whom Milcah bare unto him: and I put
the ring upon her nose, and the bracelets upon her hands.
And I bowed my head, and worshipped the LORD, and 48
blessed the LORD, the God of my master Abraham, which
had led me in the right way to take my master's brother's
daughter for his son. And now if ye will deal kindly and 49
truly with my master, tell me: and if not, tell me; that I
may turn to the right hand, or to the left. Then Laban 50
and Bethuel answered and said, The thing proceedeth
from the LORD: we cannot speak unto thee bad or good.
Behold, Rebekah is before thee, take her, and go, and let 51
her be thy master's son's wife, as the LORD hath spoken.
And it came to pass, that, when Abraham's servant heard 52
their words, he bowed himself down to the earth unto the
LORD. And the servant brought forth jewels of silver, 53
and jewels of gold, and raiment, and gave them to Rebekah: he gave also to her brother and to her mother
precious things. And they did eat and drink, he and the 54
men that were with him, and tarried all night; and they
rose up in the morning, and he said, Send me away unto
my master. And her brother and her mother said, Let the 55
damsel abide with us *a few* days, at the least ten; after
that she shall go. And he said unto them, Hinder me not, 56
seeing the LORD hath prospered my way; send me away
that I may go to my master. And they said, We will call 57
the damsel, and inquire at her mouth. And they called 58

---

48. brother's daughter. Brother is used in the sense of 'near
kinsman.' Bethuel was nephew to Abraham. Cf. xxii. 20–22.

51. take her, and go. It seems strange to us that Rebekah is
not consulted, at any rate till *v.* 58, but such is the custom in the
East.

53. jewels of gold. A formal betrothal in the East is always
accompanied by the giving of presents to the bride's family. The
practice goes back to the primitive custom of buying a bride.

Rebekah, and said unto her, Wilt thou go with this man?
59 And she said, I will go. And they sent away Rebekah
their sister, and her nurse, and Abraham's servant, and his
60 men. And they blessed Rebekah, and said unto her, Our
sister, be thou *the mother* of thousands of ten thousands,
and let thy seed possess the gate of those which hate them.
61 And Rebekah arose, and her damsels, and they rode upon
the camels, and followed the man: and the servant took
62 Rebekah, and went his way. And Isaac came from the
way of Beer-lahai-roi; for he dwelt in the land of the
63 South. And Isaac went out to meditate in the field at the
eventide: and he lifted up his eyes, and saw, and, behold,
64 there were camels coming. And Rebekah lifted up her
eyes, and when she saw Isaac, she lighted off the camel.
65 And she said unto the servant, What man is this that
walketh in the field to meet us? And the servant said, It
is my master: and she took her veil, and covered herself.
66 And the servant told Isaac all the things that he had done.
67 And Isaac brought her into his mother Sarah's tent, and
took Rebekah, and she became his wife; and he loved
her: and Isaac was comforted after his mother's death.

---

58. I will go. It was a venture of faith on the part of Rebekah
comparable to that of Abraham.

59. her nurse. In xxxv. 8 her name is called Deborah, and she
lived apparently to a great age.

62. from the way of Beer-lahai-roi. Cf. xvi. 14. But the
reading is uncertain, and the LXX 'through the wilderness to
Beer-lahai-roi' may be right. Possibly Isaac had gone to meet the
servant on his return.

63. to meditate. The word is a poetical one and has several
meanings. Possibly 'to lament.' From the fact that Abraham is
not mentioned on the servant's return, it is supposed that he had
died in the meanwhile. If so, there is a good deal to be said for
the emendation in *v.* 67 'after his father's death' for 'after his
mother's death' (lit. 'after his mother').

64. she lighted off the camel: as a mark of respect.

65. she took her veil. In Eastern weddings the bride is always
veiled. Compare the Latin *nubere*='to marry' (of a woman),
lit. 'to take the veil.'

APPENDIX ON THE EARLY
NARRATIVES OF GENESIS

No one in these days can read thoughtfully through the first eleven chapters of Genesis without being confronted with the question, How am I to understand the narratives contained in these chapters? Are they history or folk-lore? Are they historically or scientifically true? If not, are they not largely discredited? Can they really be regarded as the inspired word of God?

If we try to answer these questions we must first get clear in our minds what we mean by the words 'truth' and 'inspiration.' To say that an event is historically true means that it has actually occurred. But there is a sense in which a truth may be expressed or conveyed in terms that are pictorial rather than literally accurate. Indeed it is conceivable that there is a truth which cannot adequately be expressed in terms of human language. We cannot confine truth within the limits of what is literally accurate.

Similarly with regard to inspiration, we must beware of hedging it in too closely. If we think of it as God's infallible message revealing an absolute and eternal truth without qualification of any kind, then it is indeed difficult to believe that Genesis, or indeed the Bible as a whole, is inspired. There is so much in it that conflicts with the evidence of our senses as arrived at by the exercise of those faculties of intelligence which God has given us. But we cannot eliminate the human element in inspiration. God uses man's mind as the vehicle of inspiration, and the personality of the man has a real influence on the form in which the inspired message is delivered. So inspiration, as the Christian understands it, differs widely from the Greek idea as expressed in the conception of the Sibyl uttering words of which she has no consciousness herself, or of the priests of Apollo intoxicated by mephitic vapours, or of the speaking oaks of Dodona. It means that a human mind has laid hold of a God-given message, and transmitted it in the terms of his own personality.

It is the special privilege of the Jews that they were the people which God chose as the medium through which He should reveal Himself to man. So they were in a sense an inspired nation. God's revelation began with Abraham, and continued till Christ came into the world, born of a Jewish mother. It was imparted in various ways, through the experience of history, through the life story of individuals and through the thoughts of prophet, psalmist and philosopher. So true is it that God spake of old time 'by divers portions and in divers manners' (Hebr. i. 1).

But the Bible does not commence with the call of Abraham and the beginning of the Jewish people. It goes right back to the beginning, and gives in bold outline some account of the story of primitive man. It is this story which forms the subject of Genesis i.–xi.

Clearly these narratives are not historical as we reckon history. No one for instance could write a history of Creation, for no human eye saw the great process unfolding itself. So we seem at first sight to be reduced to two alternatives: either the stories form a direct revelation from God, or they are another variety of the numerous legends about early man current among peoples all over the world, and enshrined in the folk-lore tales that have lately received so much attention from scholars. But a little reflection will shew that neither of these alternatives is altogether satisfactory.

In the first place, taking the Bible as a whole, it would be difficult to find any parallel to a revelation from God of a scientific or historical character. Such revelations are indeed claimed in the religious books of other faiths, as for instance in the Koran, but they seem to be absent from the Old Testament. God uses the lessons of history and of nature, but they are the lessons of human experience.

And again God has given us our reason as a gift to be used, and quite frankly our reason rebels against the literal acceptance of such stories as those of Creation, the Fall, or the Flood. We find it difficult to believe that the world and all that is in it really came into being through an orderly succession of separate creative acts performed by an Architect working from outside during a period of six days, whatever 'day' may mean, or that all the evil in the world arose from a serpent tempting the first woman to eat a certain forbidden fruit, or that there ever could have been such a mass of waters on the earth as to cover the whole surface at one time including the highest mountains, or that every kind of animal could be collected into one boat and maintained for forty, or one hundred and fifty days. Nor from a moral point of view is it easy to imagine that God should ever have been jealous of the skill or power of man. So there is a good deal in these earlier chapters that from the literal point of view forms a real stumbling-block to thoughtful people.

It is therefore of importance to approach these chapters from the right angle. Probably the best way to regard the progress of God's self-revelation to men is to compare it to the education of a little child. It would be of little use to begin such education with a series of solid facts. The better way is to leave a picture in the child's mind, which may enclose as in a frame the lesson that is to be taught. And the instruction should be progressive: that is one stage should normally be completed before the next is attempted. Such was, speaking generally, Christ's method in His teaching, and such seems to have been the course of revelation as we find it unfolded in the Old Testament.

So we get quite clearly stages in man's conception of God. At first He is conceived of as an exalted type of man with human thoughts and feelings. Then gradually men put Him further above themselves, and learned more of His power, His majesty, His holiness, and His love.

So when we turn to the beginning of the Bible, we should be led from the analogy of things to expect to find there a series of pictures, rather than a sober and literal narrative of facts. In other words we should look for stories rather than history, for parables rather than authentic records. And that is exactly what the early narratives of Genesis give us.

The stories are of extraordinary interest and value, both from their literary form, and also from the lessons which they teach. And their interest is greatly enhanced by the fact that we can trace similar stories in the literature of other ancient people. Some account has already been given (pp. 5 ff.) of parallel stories of Creation and of the Flood, and for further details the reader may be referred to Driver's *Genesis* (Westminster Commentary) or Ryle's *Early Narratives of Genesis*, or, more fully, to Rogers' *Cuneiform Parallels to the Old Testament*. A comparison of these accounts shews that not only the ideas, but also the actual language of these accounts, is in many cases similar to that of the Biblical narratives. A few instances will suffice to illustrate this.

With Gen. ii. 5 compare the following extract from a version of the Creation of the world in Assyrian and Sumerian.

'The holy house, the house of the gods, in the holy place had not been made.
No seed had sprung up, no tree had been created....
No house had been made, no city had been built.'

With Gen. i. 14–18 compare the Fifth Tablet of the Story of Creation.

'He made the stations for the great gods.
  The stars, their images, as the stars of the Zodiac he fixed.
  He ordained the year, he marked off its sections....
  The Moon god he caused to shine forth, to him confided the night.
  He appointed him, a being of the night, to determine the days.'

The following extracts come from the Babylonian Flood Story.

'Pull down thy house, build a ship....
  Thy property abandon, save thy life.
  Bring living seed of every kind into the ship.'
    Cf. Gen. vi. 19.

'In its [plan] 120 cubits high on each of its side walls.
  By 120 cubits it corresponded on each side.
  I laid down its hull, I enclosed it.
  I built it in six stories.'
    Cf. Gen. vi. 16.

'Three measures of bitumen I poured over the outside.
  Three measures of bitumen I poured over the inside.'
    Cf. Gen. vi. 14.

'I brought up into the ship my family and household.
  The cattle of the field, the beasts of the field, craftsmen all of them I brought in.'
    Cf. Gen. vii. 7–8.

'When the seventh day approached
  I sent forth a dove and let her go.
  The dove flew away and came back.
  For there was no resting place, and she returned.
  I sent forth a swallow and let her go.
  The swallow flew away, and came back.
  For there was no resting place, and she returned.
  I sent forth a raven, and let her go.
  The raven flew away, she saw the abatement of the waters.
  She drew near...and came not back.'
    Cf. Gen. viii. 6–12.

'Then I sent forth everything to the four quarters of
  heaven.
I offered sacrifice.
I made an oblation on the mountain peak....
The gods smelt the sweet savour.'

  Cf. Gen. viii. 18–21.

When we read accounts such as these we can hardly
fail to recognize their kinship with some of the early
narratives of Genesis. When we attempt to account for
that kinship three alternatives arise. Either they form
part of a common tradition shared by various ancient
peoples, or the Babylonians borrowed from the Hebrews,
or *vice versa*. The first alternative would account sufficiently for the facts as far as the story of Creation is
concerned, but in the case of the Flood story it seems to
be excluded by the closeness of the parallels. The second
alternative can hardly be maintained in view of the antiquity of the Babylonian account as compared with Hebrew
literature. So the last alternative, viz. that the Hebrew
account is in some way derived from the Babylonian, has
the most probability on its side.

If this is the case, we should naturally enquire next at
what time it is likely that these stories became known to
the Hebrews. Some have thought that this happened
during the Exile, but it is highly improbable that they
were not known centuries before this. Babylonian language and culture were widespread in Palestine, as the
Tel-el-Amarna tablets attest, before the Israelite conquest
of the land, and it is not difficult to imagine that the
Israelites gradually assimilated these and other traditions.
Indeed although the story of the Flood is in its literal
sense unhistorical, it may well have arisen from the memory
of an exceptional flood in the Euphrates valley.

But we must always remember that even if we succeed in
tracing back some of the Genesis narratives to a Babylonian

source, we have not yet explained their presence in the Bible. These old records and traditions, even as they come before us in a more or less imperfect condition, are saturated with crude polytheism and unworthy motives of the gods. To take but one instance: there is all the world of difference between the Babylonian conception of earth and sky representing the two halves of the body of Tiamat split asunder by the angry Marduk, and the sublime and restrained narrative of the first chapter of Genesis.

So we may say that these early stories in Genesis are the fruit of a devout mind pondering over these ancient stories of primitive times, and guided by the Spirit of God to impart to them the lessons which have exercised so profound an influence on the thoughts of man. Here is true inspiration, not the revelation of facts and statistics, but the guiding hand of God illuminating traditions, and making them the vehicle of His teaching. The old framework is still there in such stories as those of the Evil One speaking in the form of a serpent, or the sons of God marrying the daughters of men, or the undertaking to build a tower wherewith to scale heaven. Some have gone so far as to detect a remnant of polytheism in God speaking of Himself in the plural (cf. Gen. i. 26, iii. 22). This is by no means certain, but it is not unthinkable. But however that may be, we are not bound to a literal and matter of fact acceptance of every detail in these early chapters. The more we read them the more certain we shall probably feel of their inspiration, and we shall do well to make it our principal aim both in our own study and in our teaching to bring out the moral and ethical lessons which they contain. And we shall find that some acquaintance with the early traditions of other folks will make these stories much more interesting and instructive to us.

INDEX